The new regulatory state in Germany

The New Germany in Context

Series editors: Jonathan Grix (Birmingham), Paul Cooke (University of Leeds) and Lothar Funk (University of Trier)

The *New Germany in Context* provides a forum for original research into the state of post-unity German society from a wide range of disciplinary perspectives. Since unification, Germany, and its place in the world, has undergone a period of rapid development and change. This series brings together academics from political science, economics, history and cultural studies in order to explore the legacies and debates which shape the new Federal Republic.

Other titles in the series include:

Published:

The Fall and rise of the PDS in eastern Germany
Dan Hough

Ten years of German unification: transfer, transformation, incorporation?
Edited by Jörn Leonhard and Lothar Funk

Economic transition, unemployment and Active Labour Market Policy
Corinne Nativel

Approaches to the study of contemporary Germany: research methodologies in German Studies
Edited by Jonathan Grix

East German distinctiveness in a unified Germany
Edited by Jonathan Grix and Paul Cooke

Forthcoming:

Identity creation and the culture of contrition: reconfiguring national identity in the Berlin Republic
Karl Wilds

Unification, collective bargaining and the German model of industrial relations
Steve French

German cinema after unification
Edited by David Clarke

On their own terms: German literature and the legacy of National Socialism after unification
Helmut Schmitz

The Buchenwald Child: from truth to legend
Bill Niven

The new regulatory state in Germany

Markus M Müller

THE UNIVERSITY
OF BIRMINGHAM

UNIVERSITY PRESS

First published in the United Kingdom by The University of Birmingham Press, University of Birmingham, Edgbaston, Birmingham, BI5 2TT, UK.

ISBN 0-902459-19-9

British Library Cataloguing in Publication Data
A CIP catalogue entry for this book is available from the British Library

Printed in Great Britain by Antony Rowe Ltd

Contents

Preface

Over the past two decades the industrial society of Germany has undergone dramatic transformation. Industries such as telecommunications, postal services or the railway system, once considered incapable of providing a competitive environment, have been privatised or are still in the process of privatisation. Broadcasting has long been said to be a purely public, yet state-free service, not in the least due to the potential dangers it may cause in terms of political power. But in the early 1980s private broadcasting emerged and led to the dual system of co-existence of both public and private broadcasting, each one subject to a separate regime. Finally, competitive markets such as finance (banking in particular) have recently seen enormous challenges in terms of globalisation and international regulation of financial markets. The latter development induced a major impact on German finance and its reguation.

These various aspects of politico-economic transformation in Germany raise the question, whether and to what extent they represent the rise of a 'new regulatory state'. Certainly, privatisation and regulation are of a specific nature in Germany, quite different from the privatisation experiment in Britain or the deregulation movement in the United States of America. But to what extent does this mean that industrial societies are moving towards a common model of capitalism, a presumably 'new regulatory state'? What does this regulatory state look like, what are its characteristic features? Finally, how to account for these developments and what is the future likely to bring?

Questions such as the above are brought up in this book. It is based on original research, which has been conducted in 1998 to 2000. I would like to thank all interviewees for the insights they provided as well as a range of libraries in Germany, the United States and Britain, who have provided the necessary secondary literature. I would also like to thank my colleagues at the University of Erlangen-Nürnberg for discussion and intellectual stimulation. Similarly, colleagues at Duke University as well as the University of Exeter have provided methodological and conceptual insights, which proved extremely helpful. Friends and family have provided the necessary background.

Both the Volkswagen Foundation, Hannover, and the Anglo-German Foundation for the Study of Industrial Society, London, have provided funding for the research on which this book is based. Similarly, the

Sozialwissenschaftliches Forschungszentrum of the University of Erlangen-Nürnberg has provided resources at various stages of my research.

However, this book would not have come into existence, if my academic teacher, Professor Roland Sturm, had not continuously supported my research and writing. He pointed to the significance of the theme as early as 1997 and enabled me to conduct my research with a maximum of both academic freedom and the necessary resources. Without any doubt, I owe him my deepest gratitude. I am proud to have had a chance to work with him.

Abbreviations

ARD	Arbeitsgemeinschaft der öffentlich-rechtlichen Rundfunkanstalten in Deutschland
BAFin	Bundesanstalt für Finanzdienstleistungs aufsicht
BAKred	Bundesaufsichtsamt für das Kreditwesen
BAPT	Bundesamt für Post und Telekommunikation
BGBL	Bundesgesetzblatt
BGH	Bundesgerichtshof
BKartA	Bundeskartellamt
BLM	Bayerische Landeszentrale für Neue Medien
BMPF	Bundesministerium für Post und Fernmeldewesen
BMPT	Bundesministerium für Post und Telekommunikation
BR	Bayerischer Rundfunk
BVerfG	Bundesverfassungsgericht
BVerwG	Bundesverwaltungsgericht
BW	Baden-Württemberg
BZT	Bundesanstalt für Zulassungen in der Telekommunikation
CDU	Christlich-Demokratische Union Deutschlands
CSU	Christlich-Soziale Union
DB	Deutsche Bahn
DBP	Deutsche Bundespost
DLM	Direktorenkonferenz der Landesmedienanstalten
DPG	Deutsche Postgewerkschaft
DRP	Deutsche Reichspost
DTAG	Deutsche Telekom AG
EC	European Community
ECJ	European Court of Justice
ETSI	European Telecommunications Standards Institute
EU	Europäische Union/European Union
FDP	Freie Demokratische Partei Deutschlands
FSF	Freiwillige Selbstkontrolle Fernsehen e.V.
FÜV	Fernmeldeverkehr-Überwachungs-Verordnung
GATS	General Agreement on Trade in Services
GATT	General Agreement on Tariffs and Trade

GDR	German Democratic Republic
GWB	Gesetz gegen Wettbewerbsbeschränkungen
IMF	International Monetary Fund
ISDN	Integrated Standard Digital Network
KDLM	Konferenz der Direktoren der Landesmedienanstalten
KEF	Kommission zur Ermittlung des Finanzbedarfs der Rundfunkanstalten
KEK	Kommission zur Ermittlung der Konzentration im Medienbereich
KWG	Kreditwesengesetz
LfK	Landesanstalt für Kommunikation (in Baden-Württemberg)
LMA	Landesmedienanstalt
NDR	Norddeutscher Rundfunk
NS	Nationalsozialismus/National Socialism
NZV	Netzzugangsverordnung
OECD	Organisation of Economic Co-operation and Development
RB	Radio Bremen
RegTP	Regulierungsbehörde für Telekommunikation und Post
RfStV	Rundfunkstaatsvertrag
RGBL	Reichsgesetzblatt
RIM	Reichsinnenministerium
RRG	Reichs-Rundfunk-Gesellschaft
SDR	Süddeutscher Rundfunk
SFB	Sender Freies Berlin
SPD	Sozialdemokratische Partei Deutschlands
SR	Saarländischer Rundfunk
SWR	Südwestdeutscher Rundfunk
TDSV	Telekommunikationsdienstunternehmen-Datenschutz-Verordnung
TKG	Telekommunikationsgesetz
TKV	Telekommunkation-Kundenschutz-Verordnung
TUDLV	Telekommunkation-Universaldienstleistungs-Verordnung
VAT	Value-Added Tax
WDR	Westdeutscher Rundfunk
WIK	Wissenschaftliches Institut für Kommunikationsdienste
WTO	World Trade Organisation

Part I:

Theoretical foundation and analytical framework

1

Introduction

There had long been a myth in social science. *Capitalism* was assumed to form a singular unit, representing a more or less homogenous concept of organising economic and social life. This tradition of reducing capitalism to a variation of (socio-economic) 'system' is present in both Weberian and Schumpeterian as well as Marxian and Neo-Marxian thinking, such as Immanuel Wallerstein (1974). However, even before the breakdown of socialism in Eastern Europe, three particular puzzles suggested that capitalism is more of a broad category, allowing for considerable diversity within. First, the *performance* of capitalist economies differs enormously (Hart 1992). If capitalism worked everywhere and always according to the very same principles, we would rather expect economic and social convergence in all capitalist countries. Second, when looking at divergencies of capitalist performance more thoroughly, we often observe quite different forms of *reaction* to imminent *crises*, be they economic, social or political in nature (Katzenstein 1978: 3–22; Gourevitch 1986). Thus, it seems fair to assume that there is *no* singular mechanism governing capitalist economies, which leads directly to the third puzzle: capitalist countries display a broad range of specific internal *institutional arrangements* of state–economy relations, within whose boundaries political, societal and economic players behave very differently (Hall 1986). Business, labour and the state not only have unique positions in their respective interaction, but they are also organised country-specific, which can be seen, for instance, when analysing 'corporate governance' in industrial societies. It is hardly surprising that *capitalist diversity* (Wilks 1996) has become a prominent concept to describe both institutional diversity as well as differences in the behaviour of players not necessarily induced by institutional incentives (e.g., Vogel 1996: 25). The concept's analytical use is not limited to cross-national comparison, but extends to a chronological perspective as well. That is, capitalist societies change over time, assigning new roles and meanings to their respective institutions and players within.

Despite such fundamental divergencies within market-based economies, capitalist countries have also experienced similar challenges and, even more interesting, they appear in specific cases to have reacted similarly, too. One of these cases is the reaction of governments to the problems of the *welfare state*, whose budgetary consequences have slipped out of politicans' hands. In the 1970s, it was rather fashionable to predict that the fiscal crises of almost all advanced industrial societies would eventually lead to a 'crisis of legitimacy' (*Legitimationskrise*) ultimately causing the breakdown of capitalism (O'Connor 1973). The main argument of this variation of Neo-Marxism, that the welfare state, being primarily responsible for the rising fiscal burden of capitalist democracies, will ruin the economic system as a whole is neither new or original (e.g., Caporaso and Levine 1992: 55–78; Wagner 1911), nor has it come true. Rather, Western capitalist democracies have changed to cope with these economic problems and so far, they have preserved their market-based economies. Governments cut back expenditures and altered the role of the state in their respective economies (Grimm 1996; Moran and Prosser 1994). These adjustments have followed different paths and, what is of equal interest in this context, occurred within different periods of time. That means that where there had been similar recipes chosen by governments, these policies were implemented at quite dissimilar rates at different points in time. Nevertheless, capitalist democracies did precisely what they were not supposed to be able to do (Vogel 1996: 40), i.e., the presumed logic of capitalist democracy has everywhere been proved wrong by a policy of *containing* the welfare state.

In short, while there is considerable diversity within the capitalist world, there is also some common ground for policy-making, provoking similar management of crises – at least in some instances. One of these instances is the *rise of new regulatory regimes* governing state-economy relations in the past two decades.

In the 1980s and thereafter, most, if not all, advanced industrial societies have come to the conclusion that not all of their activities have to be conducted on a basis of fiscal redistribution. This latter idea belongs to the old concept of the *Keynesian welfare state*, intervening directly when social or economic problems appear. There is, however, another way of mastering these problems without reaching into the people's pockets by taxation, and that is *regulation*. Even though this alternative had always been available to policy-makers, it has only recently gained new attention and great political appeal. One reason, why the public has not always been aware of the kind of 'public policy revolution' that has been going on for two decades, might be a conceptual misunderstanding. Paradoxically, the ubiquitous phenomenon of *deregulation* refers to the fundamental reform of *regulatory policies* accomplished since the 1970s in the United States, early 1980s in Britain, and early 1990s in Germany. In fact, the appropriate term would be *re-regulation*, as several scholars suggest (Vogel 1996; Majone 1996b). The reform and *revival*, of regulatory instruments in advanced industrial countries consist of both a change of regulatory methods (policy tools) as well as an expansion into new fields of regulation, such as telecommunication or utilities, where there had been a quite different approach of state economic policy before. Thus, it could well be argued that a certain 'spill over' of regulatory reform has taken place.

In this work, I will demonstrate that the 'regulatory state' is neither *the new* response to economic crises, as suggested by Ayres and Braithwaite (1995: 11), nor is it a phenomenon exclusively found in the Anglo-American world. Rather, 'regulation', as well as 'the state' *regulating* both economic and social issues, have existed in Germany – as well as elsewhere – since the emergence of modern statehood (Machlup 1952). What has changed dramatically, however, is the historical appearance of the regulatory state, i.e. its concrete manifestation in reality as well as its extension to areas formerly reserved for public monopolies. In fact, the dramatic shifts that have occurred in some countries, especially in Britain, during the past two decades, provoked the conclusion that there is *a* 'new regulatory state' (Ayres and Braithwaite 1995), as public policy *by regulation* has become a most important, widespread, and successful instrument of economic policy. To what extent Germany has experienced similar developments in recent years and moreover, whether the spread of these policy innovations is equally suitable for the German political and economic system, remains to be studied as follows.

However, the concepts of 'capitalist diversity' and 'the regulatory state' suggest more than the view that there are specific state–societal arrangements, forming a politico-economic order. This would only result in a revival of the debate on (neo-)corporatism versus pluralism. In fact, it seems that two lines of discussion have evolved. Whereas the analytical tool of 'policy-network' has successfully been applied in the study of state and interest group relationships, thus substantially informing the above debate on the corporatism versus pluralism dichotomy, new interest in the re-organisation of state activities and particularly its relationship with society and economy as a whole has generated new attention directed at the issue of 'regulation'. As a considerable part of my work is devoted to the theory of regulation and the theory of the regulatory state, I shall not go into too much detail. However, what distinguishes this second line of discussion from the first is its heuristic perspective: instead of inquiring into the relative position of interest groups and state players in the political struggle for or against certain policies, ultimately aiming at finding the most powerful among them, the theory of the regulatory state raises the question of how *the state* has adjusted to its very role in the economy and in society, particularly in view of both socio-economic challenges on the one hand and limited fiscal resources on the other. The hypothesis to be tested is: to what extent *regulation* has replaced *redistribution* and, by the same token, whether the *Keynesian welfare state* has been transformed into a *new regulatory state* (Majone 1996a, b).

Many interesting questions follow from this hypothetical approach to an analysis of current developments in the political economy of advanced industrial societies. Since I have assumed in this work that the regulatory state has always existed in modern industrialised countries, and thus can only replace *functions* of the Keynesian welfare state, there is one major puzzle to be resolved: How can we account for these regulatory changes? This question has two components. The first is: what kind of change is there, i.e. what elements constitute the 'new regulatory state' and therefore the new *regulatory regimes*? The second component refers to the causes for this change. While I have already noted that there is a more general rationale for replacing welfare state policies by less costly regulatory strategies, this cannot completely explain why there is regulatory reform in some areas and regulatory agony in others. In other words, the 'new regulatory state' does not extend to all fields of policy-making, not even to all those where favourable pre-conditions for regulatory reform exist.

Whereas there has been a long and intense debate on regulation, regulatory regimes and the regulatory state in Anglo-Saxon and Anglo-American countries (e.g., Seidman and Gilmour 1986; Sunstein 1990; Rose-Ackerman 1992), the German branch of political science has almost ignored this very interesting issue. However, in the meantime, a couple of case studies have appeared (e.g., Dyson 1992; Leaman 1994; Héritier *et al.* 1994). These are important as they aim at linking an international theoretical approach to the study of one important country.

This work attempts to provide a comprehensive study of the regulatory state in Germany, covering the period between the late nineteenth century, when regulatory policies were first theoretically researched and *consciously* implemented, and contemporary Germany. As I will explain in the next chapter, the 'regulatory state' is *only* used as an analytical tool that helps to classify and understand one important side of statehood (*Staatlichkeit*). It is a concept, I believe, with enormous heuristic value as it uncovers an under-researched aspect of state activity, especially in Germany. According to my concept of the 'regulatory state', it is not, however, supposed to describe the contemporary political economy in Germany as a whole. Regulation has been in existence for a considerable time, it is only its historical form (visible as *regulatory regimes*) that has changed. Whether its most recent version deserves to be labelled as a 'new regulatory state' remains to be discussed in this work.

My 'roadmap' will therefore be as follows. First, the explanation of the research design for this multi-case country study, incorporating relevant elements of the theory of regulation and the theory of the regulatory state (chapter two). Then, a brief survey of how market structures emerged in German history (chapter three). It is important to summarise the mostly pre-regulatory beginnings of modern political economy since it is then easier to understand the further course of regulatory policies over the past century.

In part two, three major areas of regulation constitute the empirical 'core' of this work: Telecommunication (chapter four), Broadcasting (chapter five), and Banking (chapter six). The cases have been carefully chosen. Banking, for instance, was among the first business areas, where the state became involved in regulation. What makes it a particularly interesting field of study is that the banking business has always been privately and publicly owned in Germany. Telecommunication has experienced dramatic changes all over the world, but especially in Germany since the early 1990s. Until then, telecommunication, as well as postal services, had not merely been publicly owned: they were united in one single public monopoly. The rise of a new regulatory regime here is not in the least connected with the decline of public ownership in this sector. Finally, Broadcasting is extremely interesting in Germany, as it involves a wide range of aspects or variables, lending it contrasting features compared to the other cases. One of these aspects is the fact that the legislative power (and therefore the regulatory power as well) lies with the *Länder* (German states) and not with the federal government. Another variable is constituted by the involvement of cultural and social concerns (e.g. *Grundversorgung*) that have played a major role in all efforts to reform public (and later also private) broadcasting.

The chapter on regulatory culture and style (chapter seven) in part three of this work, will draw some conclusions from the case studies in part two. In particular, it will answer the question how regulatory change is brought about in the areas studied and therefore, what reasons can be found for cross-sectoral variations of regulatory design. Bringing together sector-specific results provides a more comprehensive picture of the 'regulatory state' in Germany, its potential and its restrictions.

2

Theory

As there is a 'bewildering variety of meanings' (Ogus 1996: 1) of the term *regulation*, I will start with the clarification of this central concept. It will be necessary to restrict the wide range of possibilities and choose between the plethora of different opinions[1], as the concept of regulation cannot be used in a scholarly manner without reference to a particular theoretical background, including quite a few normative assumptions. That holds for *regulatory regimes* and the *regulatory state* as well, even though their scope is, of course, directly derived from the very term 'regulation'.

After this more general, but nevertheless absolutely crucial theoretical description of what kind of phenomenon this study will deal with, I will present the research design. To find answers to the question of what accounts for regulatory change in the German political economy, it will be necessary to accomplish two steps: first, to define and operationalise indicators for *change*, and second, to set up 'hypotheses' (called here *topoi*) on the *causes* for change to be traced in the course of this study. Both the classification system to determine change and the set of 'hypotheses' on causes for regulatory change will be presented in the third part of this chapter. Finally, a few comments will be added on the case selection as well as the methodology applied.

a) Regulation

Regulation, as most would understand the term, is to be located in the sphere of government–industry relation. It describes the way state actors, the *regulators*, shape and interfere with market processes (Harris and Milkis 1996: 24). In that sense, regulation is an integral part of political economy as an academic discipline. However, in my opinion, this view puts too much emphasis on the formal aspect of regulation; as if all of the government–business interaction was 'regulation'. Moreover, even if we were to simply accept such a sweeping definition of the concept, what would we gain analytically? The categories 'state' and 'market' are too broad to provide for a sensible analytical and conceptual framework. Neither of these two 'blocks' is monolithic, at least not in Western advanced industrial countries. Rather, both consist of complex structures defined by institutions, each one being a potential actor (Vogel 1996: 20). The 'naive' understanding of regulation as something that goes on between government and industry also assumes a certain kind of dichotomy between the state and the market. Both entities are, however, less clear-cut than the conceptual distinction suggests. The boundary between them seems rather flexible, being subject to continuous research itself. New institutional arrangements between state, society and market show up time and again, surprising both those who have already abolished the distinction as obsolete (such as system theorists) and those, who have tried to 'revitalise' the concepts in a more or less traditional way. However, what we see is a continuous change of this boundary between state, society and market, a fact that has encouraged some scholars to view the 'change' not as a problem of definition, but as a characteristic aspect of *statehood* in general (Mitchell 1991). In short, conceptualising 'regulation' technically as simple hierarchical administration by the state, dealing with economic or societal matters (*Eingriffsverwaltung*), misses the point as it cannot help determine the research object in any manageable way. We need a more substantial approach to understanding regulation.

Returning to the starting point presented above, we can take it a little further. Is regulation about political economy, i.e. state–economy relations? What about society? In fact, a substantial share of government regulation affects 'social' issues, and, for that matter, society at least to an equal extent as the economy. In short, whereas we may accept 'the state' – i.e. its various institutions as regulatory agents – as the one side in regulatory activities, I think that defining 'economy' as the other side does not go far enough, because it ignores society. Therefore, we need to replace the politico-economic perspective on regulation by a *statal–societal view*. The market, as well as 'the economy' as a whole, is part of society. In this context, there is no tripartite logic (state – economy – society), but a simply bipolar one (state– society/market).

What is it that brings about a higher degree of closeness between society and the economy, compared to both of them versus the state? The answer is short: society/economy and the state constitute two very different spheres of action, with quite different conceptions of rights and duties of players, realms of autonomy and hierarchical relationships. Jurisprudence distinguishes between two realms of law, one being *civil law* (society/economy), the other being *public law* (state). Whereas the first assigns the same rights and duties to all individuals and groups, treating them as equal and free players[2], the second realm of law follows a different logic, where there are hierarchies of power and of (legitimate) interests. Ogus (1996: 1–2) has coined these two spheres of action as the *market system* and the *collectivist system* respectively. This terminology shows why the economy may be treated as nothing more than a part of society[3]: as the market system is characterised as being the sphere of individual and group freedom, where everyone is engaged in pursuing his or her personal goal (Ogus 1996: 1), economic activity fits in perfectly. Production and distribution of goods and services, and all activities seen as being part thereof, follow the same logic as all (other) social interaction. This might sound like a legalistic approach to social science. However, law has always fundamentally defined actors' behaviour, be they statal or societal. Notwithstanding differences between Roman law and common law, legal relationships between individuals and societal groups (i.e. outside the *collectivist system*) follow the same logic in basically all Western industrial societies. This might neglect the problem of *power* relations, but it does say a lot about the *rules* according to which social interaction happens. Where the *rule of law* is in effect, and we may assume this to be the case in all Western countries, differences of power relations and their change over time result not so much from non-compliance with these rules, but as a consequence of their continuous, successful use.

Regulation somehow works inbetween the two spheres of the *market system* on the one hand and the *collectivist system* on the other. However, before the concept of regulation can be defined more thoroughly or more precisely, before we may determine the form of *governance* regulation represents, the more fundamental problem of the constitution of society and economy needs to be tackled. The primary question to be addressed in this context is: does the state create society and the market or vice versa? The Anglo-American perspective on this problem is probably very different from a continental European one. But the question is not just philosophical, it is legal and political as well. One school of thought takes free societal interaction, which includes all economic activities, as given and derives governance from it, as almost 'residual', by setting apart *basic rules* from *interventionist rules* (Posner 1973). Basic rules, in the Anglo-Saxon tradition of law, include all the rules of the common law. In the Roman law tradition, this would equal the civil law codes, i.e. the laws governing legal relationships between private individuals. These basic rules are somehow selected by the market (Field 1981: 175), that is, the structures of basic rules exist because they have proven efficient and necessary in every-day life. What remains for political governance are interventionist rules, i.e. 'regulation', understood, to borrow Vogel's (1996: 9) definition, as 'an essential mechanism of public control over private sector behaviour'.

This perspective brings about at least one fundamental insight that improves our conceptual understanding. Regulation is *not* 'all of law' (DeMuth 1983: 263), and common law (civil law) is to be excluded in particular. The general rules of civil law follow a distinct logic characterised by the establishment of 'boundaries for acceptable conduct within which individuals are free to gauge their actions or negotiate joint actions with others' (DeMuth 1983: 276). That is, they set standards rather than stipulations of conduct, they consist of general guidelines rather than prescriptions of exact terms of relations among individuals (von Hayek 1973, 1976, 1979). Ultimately, general (or basic) rules are self-evident and, in a sense, 'natural', as liberal social life will always need them as a basis for reliable and continuous free social interaction.

However, this view leaves us with a paradox, in that the market is created by these rules and, at the same time, is their creator. As argued by Field (1984), Weber (1958) or Polanyi (1944), market rationality cannot account for the rules required to make that rationality work. Another school of thought therefore accepts the 'defining power' of basic rules, but it cannot accept that there has always been a market to generate such rules. A different conceptual distinction is proposed, i.e. *constitutive rules* versus *regulative rules* (Rawls 1955). The former – while essentially equal to the basic rules concept, without accepting the idea of an *a priori* market – serve as constraints for the 'market game' (Field 1984: 685), even constituting (social and economic) order itself. Why is there a need for these rules? Because otherwise unsanctioned maximisation of self-interest by free individuals will lead to anarchy (Parson 1937). Therefore, it is fair to conclude that the market, viewed as a place of institutionalised free social interaction with economic goals, only comes into existence by the very acting of all actors in accordance with the rules, i.e. is virtually constituted by them. The core of the constitutive rules are the principles of civil law, determining, for example, when a person is entitled to compensation for injuries caused by others (*tort law*), which follows from the freedom of contract (*law of contract*), fiduciary obligations, forms of (private) organisation and others (Ogus 1996: 15–20). The state and its jurisprudential institutions, i.e. the justice system, enforce compliance of societal players and ensure legal adjustment to present and future needs (*Rechtsfortbildung*). However, even where this adjustment is (partly) accomplished by legislative bodies, it primarily serves no partisan or other political interests.

The constitutive rules establish a framework, which fundamentally defines the working of the market system. There are no collective goals in this system, (at least to the extent that the state provision of a legal enforcement mechanism does not qualify). However, even in neo-liberal economic thinking the market system – here viewed only in its economic function – is not immune from *internal* dangers, caused by what could be called 'private law failure'. That is, the paradox of the market system is that its legal system, private law, allows market players to behave in a way, which does not violate market system rules (civil law), yet slowly erodes market system functions. Partly, this is so because players in the market do not care about the future of the whole system, thus aiming at gaining powerful positions in order to eventually free themselves from the burden of competition. Cartelisation and trusts are prominent examples. Partly, however, there are products and services which genuinely impair competition, e.g. due to exceedingly high costs for a second grid (electricity, railways, gas, etc.). Whereas the latter describes the well-researched phenomena of natural monopolies, (certain) public goods and (certain) externalities, the first is about anti-competitive practices in general (Müller 1996). As the price mechanism is fundamentally endangered in situations of absence of competition, all of the cases described above put market sustainability in danger.

There is, however, a second problem fundamentally embedded in the market system – as both an economic and social sphere. The lack of collective goals – and respective mechanisms of the constitutive rules to pursue such goals – might cause societal dissatisfaction with market system results. Even though the 'invisible hand' of the market is usually considered to produce the best results possible, there is a wide range of instances, where society wishes to see modifications (e.g., Ogus 1996: 46–54; Francis 1993: 10–21). In some cases, such 'unfair' results originate from uneven (economic or social) power relations, be it labour contracts between employers and employees, be it parental custody of children. The market system's 'blindness' for collective concerns does not impair competition, i.e. market sustainability in an economic sense. However, it might contribute to erosion of societal loyalty and support for a market-based economy.

In short, the market system as ordered by the civil law principles of the constitutive rules displays *economic* and *non-economic* hazards, which cannot be cured within that framework. These problems do not exist in all (economic or non-economic) sectors of the market system as they originate mostly from sector-specific conditions. No matter how efficient they are otherwise, nor how crucial they are to make the market system work in general, the constitutive rules need external intervention to provide for a remedy.

That remedy is provided by *regulative rules*. They do not define the market game itself, but rather govern specific issues at the rule-maker's discretion. These rules do not constitute the market, at least not in the sense that they are absolutely necessary to uphold the continuous play in the market in the first place. Often, they simply provide answers to open questions, which arise in the course of action in the market, but which can be solved in quite different ways. Some of these open questions can be as dramatic and dangerous as described above. Nevertheless, regulative rules might be considered to overlap with constitutive rules insofar as their *goal* may be to make a certain kind of market work, e.g. fulfilling certain (public) tasks. However, the goals for regulative rules are set sector-specifically at the discretion of the rule-maker. What is very specific about the aim(s) of regulatory rules is that they *always* refer to the ***politically negotiated** public interest*. That is what shall be defined as *regulation*: circumscribing those government interventions in the realm of autonomous societal interaction, which, referring to the *politically defined* common good or the public interest, alter all or certain processes in the socio-economic sphere (*market system*) by introducing 'artificial' incentives or disincentives (similarly Vogel 1996: 9; Francis 1993: 1–2).

For example, the price system in markets as a major mechanism to facilitate exchange of products and services is not replaced, but intentionally and exogenously altered by government regulatory policies such as price caps or capital investment requirements. While such instruments of *economic regulation* have mostly indirect consequences for consumers and workers in the respective industry, *social regulation* is often more visible to the man in the street: safety belt requirements in cars, speed limits on highways or equal opportunity requirements for employers. Nevertheless, 'visibility' is not a reliable indicator for the distinction between economic and social regulation, due to two reasons in particular. First, the regulatory instruments applied in certain fields depend on the complexity of the issue at stake. Therefore, granting market entry to new competitors in the telecommunication business, for instance, is a fairly visible measure of economic regulation, whereas the tightening up of safety requirements for consumer products might be an invisible change of social regulation for consumers, who nevertheless benefit from it. As complexity varies within both social and economic regulation, so does visibility. Second, the boundaries between economic and social regulation are less clear-cut than often assumed. Public opinion as well as scholarly debate tend to view social regulation as benefiting society, while economic regulation is often considered to benefit business (Viscusi *et al.* 1996: 3–5). And even though there are different goals as well as regulatory techniques and players in the two forms of regulation, it must be emphasised that both economic and social activities are fundamentally equal in that they both belong to the sphere of free social interaction (*market system*). Moreover, measures of social and economic *regulation* overlap or have (indirect) effects on each other. Differentiating between economic and social regulation provides therefore little heuristic and analytical value.

Regulation (or regulative rules), however, do not only refer to what state players apply as instruments to exercise public control. This includes institutional arrangements to make those instruments work, too. That means in particular the setting up of *regulatory institutions*, be they governmental departments (ministries), independent agencies or other organisational bodies, created or supported by regulatory policies. These institutions do not exist independently from the market order created by the constitutive rules. However, they are not necessarily and completely bound by them. Rather, constitutive rules establish a framework for market order, open to sectoral modification by the action of the regulatory institutions only to the extent that the principle of social interaction *per se* is not violated.

The *characteristics* of regulation, as conceptionalised for the purposes of this study, follow partly direct from the above statements and partly as a consequence of them. In short, *regulation*:

- is a rule-based ***state activity***; pure forms of self-regulation are excluded
- is ***sector-specific***, be it economic or social
- is bound by a politically defined ***public interest***
- ***reaches into the market system*** and partly supersedes the otherwise applicable civil law rules, sometimes using private law tools, yet still and ultimately based on public law competence

These characteristics need further explanation. First, conceptualising regulation as a rule-based state activity demarcates the term not only from self-regulatory arrangements, but also from governmental 'casework' policies. Both claims are crucial yet contestable restrictions, demanding justification. By 'rule-based' I intend to exclude governmental intervention directed towards isolated cases, e.g. subsidies to rescue a specific firm from bankruptcy, or (discretionary) macroeconomic and industrial policies, such as (regional or sectoral) investment programmes. Regulation aims at sustaining *market* order (Wilks 1996: 538), thereby altering the order created by the constitutive rules of the market system, in order to promote the public interest. Macroeconomic policies as well as specific 'rescue measures' have only indirect implications for market orders.

The reason why self-regulatory arrangements are to be excluded in the following is very different from the 'market order' argument. In fact, self-regulation and the institutions it produces sectorally, such as professional associations supervising professional training and standards, often constitute a 'framework without which markets would collapse into disorder' (Ayres and Braithwaite 1995: 14). However, 'pure' forms of self-regulation – *pure* being the operative word in this context – are merely a phenomenon of the untouched *market system* as created and ordered by the general rules of civil law (constitutive rules). Private professional associations are just as much such a phenomenon as private cartels. As argued above, the latter, among others, might be considered quite problematic in terms of market sustainability; nevertheless, they are spin-offs of the market. Regulation, however, is separated from purely market system processes and originates from the collectivist system. Therefore, only where such formerly self-regulatory arrangements receive either public funding or recognition, are the result of state initiatives, or where regulatory powers have been delegated to these private self-regulatory institutions, are they 'lifted' out of the market system to a certain extent. Then these arrangements display some degree of state involvement, so they no longer remain in full accordance with the general rules of the market system, thus qualifying as regulation. In advanced industrial societies, most significant 'self-regulatory' arrangements fall into this category.

Regulation is sector-specific due to reasons suggested by the potentially dangerous economic and non-economic problems, not addressed or even sometimes caused by the framework created through constitutive rules. There is no need to suspend all market system rules, just because they produce unsustainable or socially unacceptable results in certain areas. Moreover, the causes for apparently dysfunctional system behaviour are quite different. They may not merely vary within economic sectors from industry to industry. Also different sections of social life display varying forms of 'civil law failure'. Nevertheless, there are certain cross-sectoral cases as well. In the economic sector, these are anti-competitive practices in particular, demanding *horizontal regulation*. For instance, cartelisation is a phenomenon, whose attractiveness does not fundamentally vary with the sector of industry studied. Incentive variations depend, if at all, on technical differences. Therefore, horizontal regulation, i.e. *competition policy*, would be a suitable approach to cure. That leaves us with the problem of discussing the relationship between *regulation* and *competition policy* in greater detail, which will be done later in this chapter.

Regulation is always bound by the politically defined public interest. This might be the most crucial characteristic of regulatory rules. By introducing collective concerns as the ultimate aim for rule-making, the fundamental cause of 'market system failure' is addressed. After all, only a presumably 'higher' public interest may justify state interference with processes of free social interaction as ordered by constitutive rules.

For the biggest part of the history of the theory of regulation, especially in economics, the 'higher' public interest seemed absolutely plain: curing *economic* market failure, e.g. fighting anti-competitive tendencies (through competition policy) or enabling sectors with natural monopolies – where the lack of competition inhibits an efficient price mechanism – to work 'market-like' with the help of substitute institutions or rules. Social justice or fairness were not, however, considered to be causes worthwhile enough for the state to intervene. This had been a *normative approach* to regulation, as the kinds of public interest goals were theoretically defined according to a more or less complex economic theory. There is, however, an alternative route to approaching the public interest and this is offered by the *positive theory of regulation*. Developed by the Chicago School (e.g., Posner 1974; Peltzman 1976; Stigler 1971), this approach to the study of regulation aims to find out why regulatory policies in reality vary considerably from what the normative theory of regulation prescribes. Proponents of this school of thought have identified interest groups, the regulated industries in particular, to be the crucial variable, explaining why regulation does not comply with the normative theory. In other words, the Chicagoans soon discovered *rent-seeking* (e.g., Buchanan et al. 1980; Rogerson 1982), be it by the regulated, be it by administrative regulators or by politicians (e.g. Noll 1983), as a highly suitable theoretical explanation, thus building bridges to Rational Choice. By doing so, it incorporated in its approach, a specific line of substantive theory, i.e. a distinct explanation of political behaviour. In this study, however, a theoretical perspective has been chosen that is 'positive' insofar as it presupposes the *public interest* to be *defined politically*. But it does not accept rent-seeking as the *only* variable to explain the behaviour of political and societal actors. Rather, as I will show later, tests need to be carried out on a broad range of possible causes of specific manifestations of regulation, drawing on different lines of substantive theories.

Finally, for regulatory goals to be effective, modes of compliance need to be created. That is, tools are necessary to make the regulated do what the regulators intend, as defined by the public interest. These tools form the bridge between the state (collectivist system) and society (market system). Generally speaking (Ogus 1996: 2), regulatory modes of compliance are *centralised* (i.e. the state is fundamentally involved in its formulation), originating from the public sphere; they are ultimately based on *public law* (i.e. its enforcement cannot be thwarted by private agreement); and they are, to a certain extent, *directives* (i.e. individuals are compelled by the superior authority of the state). Nevertheless, regulation may well use private law instruments, such as contractual agreements. That is what makes regulation such an interesting subject to study. The nature of the modes of compliance applied by regulation distinguishes it from other forms of economic state activity: it *can* use the whole set of powerful public law enforcement mechanisms, but as its success depends on societal compliance to an extent unrivalled by alternative state–economy interference (such as public ownership or financial subsidies), regulators will carefully consider the choice of tools applied. In that sense not only the public interest, but also the choice of instruments (public law, criminal law or civil law) may be subject to political bargaining, including the regulated as a negotiating partner.

Regulation may be defined according to what it is. It may, however, also become a more accessible concept to students of government and of political economy when separated from what seems similar or equal. After providing for the first in the sections above, I will now attempt to clarify the differences between regulation and a choice of politico-economic terms, which appear as close conceptual cousins.

Regulation, competition policy and *Ordnungspolitik*

Differentiating between the concepts of regulation, competition policy and *Ordnungspolitik* is necessary not only with regard to the German case. All three concepts refer to fundamental government intervention into the sphere of free social interaction – even though with a heavy bias towards economic activities. It is hardly surprising that the revelation of differences between regulation and competition policy in particular has been the subject of scholarly debate (e.g., Handler 1990). As I will later discuss, *Ordnungspolitik* represents a special German variation of conceptualising the role of the state in the economy. As the theoretical debate of regulation has always been less developed in Germany than it is in America, the 'demarcation line' between the concepts of regulation and *Ordnungspolitik* has still to be drawn.

Wilcox (Schmidt 1996) once remarked that 'regulation, at best, is a pallid substitute for competition'. What becomes clear here is one notion of regulation, which merely equates regulation with competition policy. According to this line of conceptualisation, competition policy might be categorised as *horizontal regulation*, as it reaches beyond specific industries. On the other hand, *sectoral regulation* refers to the regulation of telecommunication, utilities, finance and so on. This latter specific variation of regulation aims nevertheless at the same goal as competition policy, i.e. to provide substitute rules designed to enable competition-like market processes. Sectoral regulation differs from horizontal regulation only technically, as it takes into consideration the characteristics of the industry it is designed for.

One could certainly live with a formal distinction of (sectoral) regulation and competition policy as mere variations of the same governmental policy instrument. In fact, according to the distinction between constitutive and regulative rules presented above, it seems virtually impossible to differentiate between them. This would, however, ignore an important normative element of competition policy which might help illuminate the need for *conceptual* separation.

Competition policy is not restricted to forms of antitrust measures. It reaches all market processes, and the behaviour of firms within, that are set to produce inefficient market results, e.g. excessive prices. These *anti-competitive tendencies* constitute an inherent problem for free enterprise, hence for capitalism. The market provides for incentives to adopt business strategies that aim at overcoming the uncertainties of the market game. Trusts, cartels and monopolies are the most prominent examples. In the long run, market economies, if left untouched, tend to abolish the very principle that keeps them alive: competition. However, without competition, capitalism loses all the advantages it has compared to economies based on central planning. The market itself does not provide for a cure and that is why the state steps in. What becomes clear here is that competition policy can be seen as a *necessary* addition to a set of otherwise imperfect market rules. In that perspective, competition policy might be considered a necessary part of the legal framework built by *constitutive rules*, leaving almost no discretion if the market system is to be maintained. In a way, it resembles the public provision of a functioning court system, needed to maintain the very principles the market system is based on. Viewed from this perspective, competition policy is somehow 'pre-regulatory', i.e. closer to the constitutive rules than (other) regulatory measures based on different rationales (similarly Joskow and Noll 1981: 3).

The problem is though, competition policy is not always solely directed towards keeping alive the principle of competition. In reality, anti-monopoly offices and other public bodies concerned with competition policy act according to quite different motives. They might be political, social, cultural or economic. In fact, there *is* discretion left to the respective offices and public bodies. Moreover, even where the goals are economic, this does not necessarily mean that a higher degree of 'competitiveness' is striven for. Economic efficiency can also be defined as the strengthening of big business, enhancing its potential for mergers and acquisitions, to create global players, able to use synergies and produce at low cost. In its older version, such a strategy of competition policy is based on Clark's concept of 'workable competition' (Clark 1940), thus more restrictive: firms may grow up to the point where the highest degree of productive, 'allocation' efficiency is reached. According to the debate, so-called 'wide oligopolies' can usually be considered to be that point (Kantzenbach 1967). However, in the age of globalisation, markets do not care about national borders, so anti-monopoly and cartel offices increasingly tend to ignore them, too. Moreover, production efficiency has become of secondary importance in comparison with the idea that only strong enterprises can survive in the global fight for consumers and investors.

Most West European industrial societies have a history of incorporating strategies of industrial policy into their competition policies. At least, their respective legal framework provides for 'escape clauses', to allow for industrial policy considerations to supersede plain competition-oriented policy. There also has been much theorising about the range of goals other than economic (Ferguson 1964). Not the least important has been put forward by the theory of equivalence (Bain 1968), as formulated by Edwards (1956: 4): 'Thus competition is valued for its own sake, as the economic equivalent of political democracy, and also as a necessary aid in preserving that democracy by averting dangerous extension of the power of private organizations.'

The competition principle is considered more than a necessary element of the market (rules) system; it reaches beyond the economy and fulfils other functions. Even though Edwards' statement might be understood as suggesting that competition is an inalienable part of a democratic legal framework, it is clear that competition is *not only* about keeping the market system alive: it is also necessary to protect the state, understood here as a body politic, and defined as comprising both public institutions and the people providing for their legitimacy.

This second line of thought, assigning quite different functions to competition, hence offers a multiple rationale for competition policy and implies that competition policy uses the competition principle as a vehicle to direct market forces according to political, social or economic motives. These motives are subject to political bargaining and therefore do not necessarily complement the otherwise not un-problematically workable market order created by the constitutive rules. Competition policy thus becomes virtually indistinguishable from regulation.

Ordnungspolitik is a highly problematic concept (Abelshauser 1991), which serves a distinct political goal in Germany. It is based on the idea that the state provides for both a general legal framework to enable market players to work in a safe societal environment, governed by the rule of law (*Rechtsstaatlichkeit*) and more specific economic and social interventions to secure market stability, steady growth and social peace. That seems to suggest that *Ordnungspolitik* covers both constitutive and regulative rules. And this does hold true but only to the extent that the term is not a neutral category. The concept of *Ordnungspolitik* is fundamentally linked to the notion of *Soziale Marktwirtschaft*, i.e. a social market economy, which obliges the state to safeguard a certain minimum standard of social justice (Müller-Armack 1976). As mentioned above both *Ordnungspolitik* and *Soziale Marktwirtschaft* have a strong normative bias: the state shall interfere with the economy, especially its institutions, rules and norms (Katzenstein 1989), but it shall keep its hands off the market itself, especially microeconomic processes (Eucken 1952). This latter point includes a certain dislike of public enterprise, which has nevertheless *not* led to the complete abandonment of public entrepreneurship. In other words, the state as an economic actor in Germany performs, according to the principle of *Ordnungspolitik*, in basically the same way as other states elsewhere in the world; this doctrine does not provide for additional instruments or tools. However, it provides for a certain normative perspective, including a whole set of political (i.e. social and economic) goals. *Ordnungspolitik* could be seen as the most comprehensive term used so far, comprising both the constitutive legal framework governing the market order, competition policy (understood as complementing constitutive rules) and regulation (understood as sector-specific intervention, aiming at a diverse range of goals). Nevertheless, one should keep in mind the normative and politico-economic bias, putting a strain on its analytical usability.

Regulation, redistribution, taxation and macroeconomic policies

The rise of the regulation debate is connected to the problems of the Keynesian welfare state. Interfering with macroeconomic processes by means of fiscal redistribution, i.e. taxing private income (economic activity) and redistributing these funds to pursue macroeconomic (business cycle) targets, has somehow reached its limits. Whether it is the rise of globalisation and international competition or whether internal causes, such as an aged population (von Weizsäcker 1999) in most Western industrial societies, have led to budgetary troubles, especially in the 1970s and thereafter (Sturm with Müller 1999), is still subject to scholarly debate. But it seems clear that there is no room for further growth; on the contrary, due to rising costs of incumbent (entitlement) programmes, the welfare state has to suffer cut-backs. The need to install reduction policies is not limited to welfare spending, including social security, but extends to subsidies and investment programmes supporting regional development and infrastructural progress or simply boosting economic growth. However, reducing fiscal redistribution means that the general level of state activity, especially with regard to society and the economy, is also reduced.

Majone (1996a, b) has come up with another view. Looking at the case of the European Union, Majone notices that the EU somehow becomes a state-like entity, but it has no chance to develop the same Keynesian welfare state attitudes, due to the above-mentioned fiscal crises of industrial societies in general. As the member states are unable to maintain their respective levels of welfare benefits, subsidies or public investments, it is highly unlikely that these countries are willing to endow the Union with the resources needed for redistribution as welfare benefits, subsidies or investments. In spite of already having funds available for regional and infrastructural measures, of which most is spent on agricultural subsidies, Brussels lags far behind when compared with the resources spent in its member states.

Nevertheless, the EU has found other ways of increasing its competence and sphere of influence: by means of regulation. To an ever greater extent, European Law, e.g. Directives, guidelines or jurisdiction of the European Court of Justice, constitutes a framework, within which the scope for national differences is constantly diminishing. Without spending money, the European Union governs to an increasing extent economic and also social policies. Majone therefore sees the EU as the prototype of a new regulatory state.

According to this logic, the Keynesian welfare state, including its policy tools, e.g. redistribution and taxation, stands in juxtaposition to the regulatory state, employing quite different instruments of policy-making, e.g. setting standards and opening up market entries. The welfare state and the regulatory state form two alternative methods of governing both the economy and society.

In fact, regulation seems irreconcilable with the idea of withdrawing resources from the private sector to allocate them for other purposes, be it economic growth, industrial policies or infrastructural development. Regulation is, as argued above, a *rule-based state activity*. It intends to alter the market order created by the constitutive rules – in accordance with the politically defined public interest. However, this might include *taxation*, as tax codes often produce new incentives for players in the private markets, thus changing their calculations. Hence, taxation belongs in the set of tools available to regulators (*regulation by taxation*), but only insofar as tax codes are consciously used to change the behaviour of players in the market and not as a means to raise public funds for redistribution.

But why cannot macroeconomic (anti-cyclical) state intervention be seen as a variation of regulatory activity? Does it not represent a form of state interference with the market, still allowing players in the market to maintain their processes of (microeconomic) exchange? Indeed, as Keynesians and Neo-Keynesians argue, the business cycle problem can be seen – just like anti-competitive tendencies – as an inherent problem of capitalism; only this time it is not a problem of individual misconduct, but of collective failure. As players on both the demand and the supply sides follow the same market signals, the general macroeconomic trend (boom or recession) grows. Markets are unable to produce stable and steady growth. If one subscribes to that perspective, anti-cyclical Keynesian policies which try to stabilise the business cycle by influencing macroeconomic indicators, fulfil a function somewhat similar to competition policy, i.e. curing a flaw in the constitutive rules framework and ultimately being a part of it. However, the consequence of this approach would also be that Keynesian macroeconomic policies do not necessarily qualify as *sectoral* regulation.

Finally, if one does not subscribe to the above, then macroeconomic 'steering' of the economy is simply an act of discretionary spending, a voluntarily employable instrument of policy-making. It is neither sector-specific, nor rule-based. If one were to include it in the working definition of regulation, the latter concept becomes virtually synonymous with 'governing'. Applying such sweeping terminology would not only ignore important conceptual differences, but most importantly, it would disguise recent developments in Western industrial societies. After all, they tend to increasingly abandon Keynesianism and fiscal redistribution so that finding an explanation of such developments becomes a part of our exercise.

Regulation and public enterprise

In all Western industrial societies states engage as public entrepreneurs. In some cases, governments, be they central, federal, state or local, operate monopolies, such as telecommunications, utilities, railways or broadcasting. In other cases, they just offer certain products and services through public enterprises (e.g. banks, insurance companies, or TV stations), competing with private businesses. Needless to say that privatisation and deregulation policies have revolutionised hitherto state-dominated industries.

Schliesky (1997: 45–93) argued that it is difficult to distinguish between regulation and public entrepreneurship since both forms of state economic activity have fundamentally equal consequences in the market system, i.e. for market system players. One could certainly view publicly-owned businesses as fulfilling the same function as regulation, i.e. sustaining the market order, in particular where private enterprises are unable to provide the supply of products or services (Stober 1989: 674). But this seems to be a normative perspective, sustained by the normative theory of regulation, which does not necessarily reflect reality.

First of all, public monopolies have to be distinguished from publicly-owned competitors in an otherwise 'free' market. Schliesky's assertion holds up here best of all. Public monopolies have traditionally been justified as a necessary departure from the rule of private enterprise, because the latter would be unable to provide a stable, fair and comprehensive supply. In other words, the state takes over all market functions and private social interaction comes to an end. Public enterprises may use civil law instruments, such as contracting, but state monopolies basically replace the market system in a specific sector. Thus, where public monopolies fully dominate the market, there cannot be regulation, as regulation requires both a collectivist system (the state) and a market system (the respective sector or industry) to interact in certain ways.

A more interesting case is the co-existence of publicly- and privately-owned businesses in one sector. Operating public businesses may well be seen as a means of regulating a specific industry, but not all cases qualify. By serving specific communities or regions, or by offering their products and services at a political price or on certain conditions, public enterprises can directly pursue a public interest, politically defined and vested in the respective statute. If the neglect of specific communities or regions, etc., is seen as a sort of market failure (which nevertheless does not endanger the system as a whole), public entrepreneurship can be considered a variation of regulation. This holds, too, where public corporations are set up to give private competitors an incentive to comply with their corporate goals, e.g. providing favourable conditions for special communities.

Nevertheless, the regulatory function of public enterprises has been somewhat diminished by competition policy. It is not in the least due to developments in EU law that public engagement in the market has become subject to scrutiny, because it has been suspected of using unfair practices: favourable conditions and the like are often subsidised by public funds. As a consequence, governments have often discontinued their entrepreneurial engagement and privatised the firms or transformed these corporations into fully equal market suppliers with no substantial difference to other market participants. What should be noted here is that the organisation of public corporations, their management and their market behaviour is not necessarily relevant to understanding regulation in the respective industry. Only where these businesses have a significant impact on the market, where they help sustain market order or effectively shape market results, do they deserve attention as elements of a regulatory regime (similarly Ayres and Braithwaite 1995).

b) Regulatory regimes and the regulatory state

Given the characteristics of regulation presented above, it seems obvious that any study of regulation is first and foremost an inquiry into the regulatory state. As regulation represents one, but non-homogenous, form of state activity, the history of regulation is also a history of statehood. In fact, this is what makes regulation a core subject for political science: the state is *still* conceived as a major agent and not just one 'arena' among many, more or less overlapping other organisational bodies of society. Regulation is one important part of statehood, and as such it is determined by endogenous and exogenous institutions, which effectively shape state-societal relations. These institutions necessarily transcend the sphere of the state (i.e. the collectivist system), at least in the sense that their actions are directed towards the outside world (i.e. the market system). That is, the state as a regulator must possess institutions, whose links to the market system are qualified to transmit the (politically defined) public interest to market system participants. This creates a quite complex structure of cross-statal and cross-societal, interlocking connections, forming something, which has been called ***regulatory regime***.

The regime concept, successfully used in the study of international relations, has been added to the conceptual tool kit for the study of regulation, probably because of some analogies to its application in international relations (Krasner 1983; Rittberger 1995): the significance of rules and norms for the behaviour of social, institutional or personal actors. That includes the special problem of complying with the rules. Notwithstanding the substantially different meaning it has in international relations, the regime concept has gained general attention throughout political science. Ironically posed, the term represents a compromise of both the rejection of state- and law-centred approaches to the explanation of social realities on the one hand and the acceptance, on the other hand, of the undeniable empirical impact of institutionalised, legal and ethical norms as a framework for social life. More positively expressed, the introduction of an international law concept into the study of social realities means returning to a more normative and constructivist attitude on social interaction. That means using a former legal term to describe those norm-loaded and more or less institutionalised complexes, which effectively influence or even determine social action.

Regardless of this more general qualification of the regime concept, the usage of *regulatory regime* in the study of regulation and the regulatory state seems rather standardised and consistent. Two lines of inquiry are joined together in the term: first, *regime orientation* and second, *regime organisation* (Vogel 1996: 20). While the first refers to regulatory goals, ultimately translating the public interest into public policy, the second extends to regulatory actors, institutions and policies involved in the regulatory process. In a formal sense, regulatory regimes describe a structure of both goals and organisation (Harris and Milkis 1996: 25), but, at least in this study, the concept is not restricted to a system of 'categorising'. Rather, it has a specific, heuristic aim: *How* does the state interfere in the sphere of free societal interaction? In what way do (regulatory) state actors build up their institutional relations with societal (hence also economic) players? Which institutions within the market system, prima facie developed independently therein, do the state actors have to confront? What regulatory goals, defined by the politically negotiated public interest, do regulators aim at and how to they realise them?

These questions show that '*interferential intensity*' (*Eingriffstiefe*) is a central point of inquiry to identify the degree of regulatory state activity[4]. The concept refers to the extent of state involvement in the sphere of free social interaction. In this context, another aspect becomes crucial: legitimation and sustainability, i.e. the problem of *regulatory balance* (similarly Viscusi *et al.* 1996: 7). What degree of state involvement is sustainable and acceptable to societal players? Which instruments of interference may *not* be used? Which sections of the sphere of free social interaction are taboo? What I would like to emphasise here is that the above-mentioned core elements of the concept of the regime in the study of regulation and the regulatory state ('orientation' and 'organisation') include a set of aspects, which of necessity bring about the need for heuristic specifications for certain concepts (such as 'interference' or 'regulatory balance').

I use the concept of *regulatory regime* in this study as an important step towards operationalisation of the regulatory state – and not just regulation. That is, I do not argue that 'regimes exist', but that the regulatory activity of state actors can quite effectively be researched by using the concept of the regime as an analytical tool, to identify and distinguish between central elements of regulation, initiated and implemented by the state. The concept necessarily transcends the sphere of statehood, extending to the market system: for state regulatory policies to become effective in the market system, they need to specifically address the market system's 'logic of action'. At the very least, the 'right' actors and institutions must be chosen at which regulatory measures are directed. In order to account for variations in these relations between systems, crossing state–society boundaries, it is necessary – at least on the operational level – to provide for an appropriate conceptual framework. Therefore, the term of regulatory regime is created as an analytical tool to fully capture regulatory action.

However, it should be emphasised that the concept of regulatory regime is not intended to expand the original research interest of this study. Still, the study of regulation is understood as the study of the regulatory state. Furthermore, the regulatory state is conceived as a manifestion of statehood, changing over time, cross-sectorally and cross-nationally. I do not aim to work out fields of regulation, such as the regulation of telecommunication or utilities, even though it is necessary to inquire substantially into these fields in order to understand concrete regulatory state action. Nevertheless, the ultimate goal is to understand modern statehood as revealed by one of its aspects, the regulatory state. The following three analytical elements of regulatory regimes should therefore be understood as an operationalisation of this study's research agenda, ultimately categorising observable elements of regulatory regimes.

Legitimacy – regulatory goals and the public interest

Legitimacy refers to the regulatory goals as defined by the public interest. These goals determine the direction of regulatory intervention by the state, ultimately putting the public interest in concrete terms. Thereby, regulatory goals *legitimise* state interference with the market system's order.

From the above it is clear that the ***public interest*** is the crucial category here. It is understood, just like the whole set of concepts discussed in this chapter (regulation, regulatory state, regulatory regime), to be an analytical instrument to capture elements of changing statehood. As the concept of public interest is used in a variety of ways, these alternatives need to be distinguished. I propose to categorise these alternatives on three levels:

(1) the public interest as a (legitimising) *reference*;
(2) the public interest as a *political goal*;
(3) the public interest as an *indicator for the winner.*

(1) On the first level, the public interest serves as a reference, which is supposed to rhetorically justify regulatory policies. For instance, proponents of protectionist regulatory norms in specific market sectors, such as utilities or insurance business, refer to standard opinions of the normative theory of regulation. According to this school of thought, some market sectors, such as those mentioned above, show characteristics which inhibit workable competition due to, for instance, natural monopolies (sector-specific market failure). When the free market order is found to be not working efficiently, regulatory measures, such as legal protection of an existing (local) monopoly, are considered necessary to maintain the provision of the common utilities (electricity, water, gas and so on).

Economic rationales, be they correct or not, such as the one above, have great normative power, thus justifying state intervention, seemingly directed towards curing sector-specific market failure. Whether the economic rationales brought forward really apply, i.e. whether their consideration represents good economic analysis of the market sector in question, is something totally different. According to Stigler's, Peltzman's and Posner's analyses of regulation in several fields, this seems often quite doubtful. However, their search for the 'real' causes of regulation, ultimately establishing the positive theory of regulation, reveals the need for distinguishing between 'regulatory rhetoric' and the true basis or rationale for regulatory activity (Joskow and Noll 1981: 1). Nevertheless, the normative theory of regulation offers a variety of rationales for regulatory intervention, which still have an enormous legitimising power (even though they might be wrong vis-à-vis the analysis of concrete cases). As well as economic justifications, other regulatory rationales may deliver suitable goals, too, legitimising state involvement, socially or culturally.

(2) The second level introduces the public interest as what it 'really' is, i.e. a *political goal*. It not only delivers a 'rationale', justifying state action (1), but there is actually an honest, if political, state intention. It *can* refer to curing market failure and increasing market efficiency, but it may also be something different (Ogus 1996: 26–54). Among these different goals are social-redistributive goals, such as supporting meritorious (*meritorische*) goods or stabilising and reducing risks for people, economic order and polity. Even protecting national industries against international competitors *can* be such a goal, thus establishing a public interest. What should be clear is the difference between level (1) and level (2). While level (1) refers to arguments and rationales, which, *correctly* or not, justify regulatory involvement, level (2) represents true goals, which, *explicitly* or not, are found to be behind regulatory policies.

The public interest, understood as a set of political goals, can be quite diverse. As argued above, there is an almost unlimited plethora of possibilities. However, in order to enable cross-sectoral and also cross-country comparison, a system of classification is needed to subsume the whole range of alternatives. In the following, three classes will be used: *efficiency*, *equality* and *security*. The first class, ***efficiency***, refers to the cure of sector-specific *market failure*. This regulatory goal is most certainly the closest to competition policy targets. The second class, ***equality***, includes re-distributive goals of regulation, at least to the extent that they are *socially* motivated and directed towards creating equal opportunities or access to resources. The difference between both classes of regulatory goals – hence of public interest – lies in the following: efficiency goals aim at securing and maintaining the functioning of market processes, equality goals are concerned with modifying market results, which, even though produced by a working market order, are conceived as unfair or antisocial. Thus equality goals demand either *ex post* remedy or *ex ante* changes, so that such an unfair market outcome is impossible from the start. The third class, ***security***, refers to *protectionism* of various kinds. For one, it includes protecting national industries (incumbents) against both international competitors *and* national challengers. Over and above that, security stretches to stabilising community and polity, for instance, by banning pornography and similar items perceived as 'ethically dangerous'. Security goals do not, therefore, contribute to market stability as do efficiency goals, nor are they meant to have a 'social' impact by aiming at re-distributive justice like equality goals; yet they might indirectly contribute to social stabilisation, even though their intention is not directed towards creating 'equality' as an ethically desirable status of society.

(3) On the third level, the public interest can be used as an *indicator* of who won the political struggle for individual or group interests. This level connects the 'true' political goal, however rhetorically justified to the public, with those who benefit from the new policy or who might at least hope for benefit. In a way, this is the most political view of the public interest, concerned as it is with *power* and *politics*. Hardly surprising then, there is already abundant literature on the theory of who (and whose interests) dominate regulatory politics and hence the regulatory policies pursued.

The Chicago School of thought (*positive theory of regulation*) has already been introduced above, with an emphasis on its heuristic intentions. At this point, the Chicagoans' approach should be appreciated as a substantive theoretical contribution, offering an explanation into how regulatory policies come into existence. Its core element is Stigler's approach of a *Capture Theory*, claiming that (economic) regulation is kept alive by certain groups who 'capture' regulatory institutions and 'demand' regulation. A market analogy suggests itself: Within the market for regulation, the state actors (regulators) offer 'regulation' which is advantageous for (certain) firms or industries. The latter make demands for such desirable 'regulation'. According to the theory, the more profitable the regulatory policy in question, the higher will be the demand for it; correspondingly, the more attractive a regulatory policy, the more likely are those who demand it, to spend resources (financial or political) on lobbying[5].

A variation of this conception emphasises the interests of the regulators and their staff (Niskanen 1971, 1994; Müller and Vogelsang 1979). *Independent regulatory agencies* are especially suitable for studying the hypotheses of this approach: their staff, who are relatively independent from political will in parliament, will most likely aim at serving the regulated industries to the best of their interest, in order to enhance their chances to get a better job there, after some time in public service. The exchange of personnel has been labelled as the *revolving door* phenomenon.

Given the high durability of regulatory regimes protecting the market sector's status quo, thus favouring the incumbents, both the *interest group* and the *public choice perspectives* above seem convincing. However, these approaches struggle to explain the regimes' changes towards liberalisation of markets or other regulatory innovations, which are not in the interest of the regulated incumbents. Even though one could argue that another interest group has taken over or that the regulators have switched sides, it seems at least equally appropriate to consider the argument of the 'classical' *public interest approach* (Francis 1993: 7). According to this view, the state, i.e. the agents acting on its behalf, actually aims at finding a solution beyond group interests. In the stricter sense, there would be no 'winner' from a regulatory policy. However, there have been variations of this approach, which emphasise the possibility of balancing out group interests with a presumably 'perfect' theoretical solution generated beyond them. According to the classification system proposed in this section, at least rational functionalism would expect the 'classical' public interest to be found at level (1), rhetorically justifying regulatory policies, but non-existent at level (2).

The three levels described so far are best understood as analytical categories that help distinguish – in the course of research – between different aspects of meaning which 'the public interest' may adopt. The first level (i.e. rhetorical justification) is intended here to keep research from being taken in by superficial rationales, often presented in public speeches and published opinions. The third level (indicating the winner) is ultimately directed towards the same target, at least in those cases where both the winner and his or her relations with the incumbent regulatory regime is obvious. But it is the second level, i.e. the search for the true political goals, however explicitly justified and however clearly explained in terms of benefits and losses, and then to be sub-classified into *efficiency*, *equality* and *security*, that will be primarily focused upon in the course of my research. These categories will foster a search for 'intentional differences' of regulatory regimes in the sectors to be studied.

Agency – regulatory institutions and actors

Regulation needs organisational form before it can be realised. That is, regulatory institutions have to be established, their regulatory tasks and competence have to be defined and finally, their daily work has to be supervised in an appropriate way. Above all, it must be clarified whether these regulators are free to define the *public interest* at will, or within certain boundaries set by another political or executive actor.

Generally speaking, regulatory institutions need to be studied with regard to two aspects in particular: first, on which level of government is the regulatory authority, which these institutions translate into public policy (similar Francis 1993: 64–65), and second, what is their relationship with other executive or political bodies? The first aspect is of special importance in federal states, such as Germany, where political power is spread over different levels of government (federal, state (*Länder*) and local). Moreover, some powers are exclusive, others are shared by different levels. And even where one level, e.g. the *Länder*, have jurisdiction over a certain issue (e.g. broadcasting), they have found it necessary, partly due to court rulings, to co-ordinate their policies in order to avoid a confusing legal non-uniformity in the country as a whole. Even though the aspect of location of regulatory authority seems to transcend the institutional question, it has a deep impact on it: corresponding to the location of authority (exclusive or shared power; federal, state or local jurisdiction, etc.) the institutional arrangement varies cross-sectorally. It also influences financial resources, supervision or staffing of regulatory institutions, at least in a broader sense.

The second aspect lies at the core of studying institutional arrangements of regulation in different sectors: what status do regulatory institutions have and what is their relationship with other executive, political and juridical bodies? This question needs to be sub-categorised to throw light on the multitude of angles to be considered. First, the *legal status* of regulatory institutions. German law provides for a variety of legal forms, ranging from ministry to public enterprise (which might even be established as a formally private law company). More generally speaking, the status varies from public to semi-public, especially if one takes into account the degree of involvement of other (private) actors. The latter and the legal form stand in mutual interrelation, as some legal forms allow for access of private actors, while others do not.

Second, the extent of *autonomy*. This refers to the degree of independence from other state organs of the regulators who, by definition, are part of the state. Most importantly, it is interesting to look at how much discretion the regulatory institution in question has in defining the public interest – or at least in choosing and assessing the tools to realise it. The extent of discretion here ultimately defines the institutional autonomy. It should be emphasised though, that regulatory autonomy is often considerably constrained by the courts (also Sunstein 1990: 111–192). Therefore, not only executive and political bodies should be considered in their relations with regulatory institutions, but also juridical bodies.

However, autonomy is not only a function of independence from other state institutions and hence with discretion for decision-making, but might also be understood as depending on the degree of 'societal participation'. That is, to what extent does the state incorporate society into its regulatory agents? And in what way? The latter question is crucial, because it makes a difference as to whether regulatory institutions have a corporatist, a pluralist or an independent-etatist structure and understanding of themselves (Francis 1993: 55–61). Correspondingly, 'semi-public' is a broad concept, that covers a whole range of different kinds of societal incorporation.

Third, *internal organisation* is another aspect to be studied. Not only is the degree of societal involvement (or incorporation of other than statal actors or staff) crucial for the decision-making process, but the formal organisation of procedures and of authority matters also. That is what internal organisation means in this context. Regulatory agencies can be structured in a variety of ways: hierarchical (according to the classical principles of executive agencies), collegial or co-operative (according to juridical bodies) or consensual (according to the 'round table' principle, requiring unanimous decision). Of course, internal organisation is not an independent aspect, but stands in direct, mutual relations with the legal status of an agency, its degree of autonomy and the degree of societal interference.

The aspects listed above are not necessarily congruent with legal categories. This study is interested in *actual* autonomy or societal involvement, not the one provided by law. Of course, the law probably delivers the most important basis for these aspects. It defines the framework, thereby, more or less, leaving enough space for manoeuvre. However, legal norms need interpretation and realisation. Both can be creative and expansive or restrictive. Furthermore, interpretation is not only a matter of judicial review (even though this is an important one), but also of agencies' practice: in order to translate legal norms of a bill or an executive order into regulatory policies, they need to be interpreted. Both judicial and agency interpretations do not necessarily concur with the legislative intention. In short, analysis of institutional arrangements in highly legalised political systems, such as Germany's, can well be gained by an analysis of law and other legal norms, but it does not have to be restricted to it.

Compliance – regulatory modes and instruments

For regulatory institutions to successfully realise their regulatory goals, they need to apply instruments of various kinds to make the regulated do what the regulators want. In order to generate compliance of the regulated with the public interest, as operationalised in the regulatory goals, *regulatory modes* need to be set up in accordance with the characteristics of both the sector market and its industry. 'Compliance' in the sense in which the term is used in this study refers to the mechanisms used to ensure compliance of the regulated.

Regulatory institutions dispose of a range of regulatory modes, which can be classified according to their *severity of interference*, i.e. the extent of state interference with otherwise free societal interaction in the sector studied. They range from persuasion and other forms of *soft regulation*, which have no immediate legal consequences in cases of non-compliance, through new or modified incentives to steer societal players' behaviour (*incentive regulation*), to legal bans and rules, which are directly enforceable. There are different possible combinations and variations of these regulatory modes while scholarly research as well as regulatory practice have already provided an insight into effective and ineffective uses thereof (also Ayres and Braithwaite 1995).

The study of why and under which conditions compliance with norms set by other actors is best achieved has consumed considerable resources in political science in general, as well as in the research on the above mentioned international regimes in particular. Even though this perspective on collective action is central to the discipline as a whole, this study is less interested in the phenomenon of compliance itself than in the *choice* of regulatory modes to foster it. Anyway, that choice can be influenced by good or bad experiences in the past, in other sectors, or even in other countries. Thus, the regulators' perception of how compliance is best achieved is a crucial aspect.

In correspondence with established research on regulation, regulatory modes shall be exclusively used as a concept for the above-mentioned perspective of *severity of interference*. Regulatory instruments, however, shall refer to the variables chosen to be controlled, such as price, quantity, market entry or market exit (Viscusi *et al.* 1996: 307–311; Joskow and Noll 1981: 3–35). Each of these variables can be controlled to a different degree of 'severity of interference'.

Regulatory regimes and the regulatory state – a short summary

The concept of regulatory regime has been introduced as an analytical tool to describe central elements of regulatory action by the regulatory state. It has thus been severely restricted in its heuristic use. After all, it is designed specifically for this study, making possible, on a more operationalised level, a comparison of regulation in different sectors. Its usage is not limited to the study of economic regulation, but this is all it will be used for in this work. However, I want to emphasise that despite the language of the above sections the theoretical design of the regulatory regime concept is wide enough to also allow for the study of social regulation.

Table 2.1 Regulatory regime as analytical concept

	Regulatory regime	
Legitimacy	**Agency**	**Compliance**
(*'what'* ?)	(*'who'* ?)	(*'how'* ?)
1. Public interest as reference	1. Legal status	1. Regulatory modes – *severity of interference*
2. Public interest as political goal – *efficiency* – *equality* – *security*	2. Degree of autonomy and independence – *relationship with other state institutions* – *degree of societal participation*	2. Regulatory instruments – *variables to be controlled*
3. Public interest as indicator for the winner	3. Internal organisation (*hierarchical, collegial, consensual*)	

Regulatory regimes are defined as a combined set of organisational, instrumental and intentional elements, established by the state. These elements are referred to by the concepts of *Legitimacy*, *Agency* and *Compliance* (Table 2.1). This conceptualisation is less focused on the procedural aspects of regulation, such as interest group influence on the political process or questions of implementation or output control. Yet it does not ignore them; it is just not built around them. The (heuristic) goal, once again, is the study of statehood and its evolution over time as well as its concrete, cross-sectoral variations. In a sense, 'regulation' as such is considered a vehicle for the study of statehood. Reducing the analysis of regulation to how *the state* regulates seems to me a considerable improvement in developing the positive theory of regulation as a testable theoretical framework, because empirical research, cross-sectorally and cross-nationally, is more substantive when comparable categories are used.

c) Explaining regulatory change

Regulatory regimes, hence the regulatory state, change with time. And yet, regimes of different sectors change at different rates and take quite different directions. Furthermore, in a cross-country comparison even the same sectors (e.g. broadcasting or telecommunications) change very differently (with time). Thus, regulatory regimes vary

- cross-sectorally
- chronologically, and
- cross-nationally.

Regulatory change can be identified on specific occasions, i.e. *upheavals*. Notwithstanding the more theoretical, if not fictitious debate on 'regime evolution' versus 'regime revolution' (Eisner 1992: 2–3; Harris and Milkis 1996: 23–25; Francis 1993: 96), it seems important to emphasise that regime change concerns all three analytical elements of the regime concept, i.e. *Legitimacy*, *Agency* and *Compliance*. After all, regulatory change can be identified as changes in these three areas of analysis, i.e. as upheavals of goals, institutions or modes. By analysing each singular aspect of 'Legitimacy', 'Agency' or 'Compliance' separately, important insight into the changes in regulatory regimes and the regulatory state can be gained and thus provide us with information on the change of statehood.

Moreover, co-relations between changes in these three aspects are of special interest. That is, for instance, when there are changes in *institutional arrangements* (*Agency*), i.e. the institutional role of the state as a regulator, do *regulatory goals* (*Legitimacy*) and/or *regulatory modes* (*Compliance*) change then, too? Co-relations provide for substantial evidence on the manner of change in regulatory states, e.g. possible or likely restrictions.

However, this study will primarily focus on occasions of change, such as upheavals. This means that the emergence of new regulatory institutions, goals or modes – or a combination thereof – will be taken as a dependent variable, needing to be explained: What accounts for regulatory change? When searching for answers to this question, there are several options available. Since methodological questions will be addressed in the next section of this chapter, there is nothing further to add here. However, I wish to present my study procedures.

Instead of setting up hypotheses to be confirmed or disproved, this work strives for an approach using topoi, which deliver a range of *possible* causes for regime change. That is, it is assumed that regime change is driven by a variety of forces, whose relative importance needs to be identified case by case. However, the result of studying possible causes of change might well be that the list of topoi is incomplete, i.e. other forces might be case-specifically more relevant. This strategy of research has already been applied by others, such as Francis (1993: 96), but it needs adaptation to both the country and the sectors studied. The topoi used in this study, if provisional, include the following.

Crisis

The first cause, which can force regulatory change, is a *crisis* in the incumbent regime (Sunstein 1990: 74–110; Owen and Braeutigam 1978). Crises can show quite diverse characteristics and may result from a range of different factors. With regard to the first, two different sorts of crises can be distinguished: *endogenous crisis* and *exogenous crisis*. While the latter refers to external events that pose a significant problem for the incumbent regime, the first concerns dysfunction of current regime mechanisms, such as ineffective incentives or sanctions. Differentiating between endogenous and exogenous crises does not, however, imply their strict separation. Rather, it seems sensible to include analytical space for a combination of both, i.e. system dysfunction interrelating with new problems caused by external shocks (e.g., Whicker 1993: 79–107). It should also be noted that some of the potential causes of regime change in the following sections might qualify as external shocks in a broad sense. They are, however, analytically separated so that 'external shock' as a term is reserved primarily for sector-specific problems. Thus, one would expect to find signs of sector-specific failure, such as collapses of incumbent firms, protests by consumers or important businesses on the demand side, or significant negative changes in microeconomic indicators of the sector studied. As we shall see, the emergence of a regulatory regime governing the banking sector in Germany in the 1930s, and another regime change later in the early 1970s, are cases in point.

Ideological change

Regulatory change can be ideology-driven (Benz and König 1997: 607). In this case, a new approach to regulating either the economy (as a whole) or a specific sector has emerged. There is, however, no immediate need for the incumbent regime to adapt to new challenges (Majone 1996a: 34; Derthick and Quirk 1985). Rather, a new set of ideas on the role of the state in the economy, be it as a regulator or be it as a public entrepreneur, demands change. Ideological shifts themselves might be caused either by a change of government (hence of the ruling party or coalition) or by fluctuation of staff within the executive, especially independent regulatory agencies. This latter aspect is not restricted to the executive board and top level executives. Depending on internal organisation, new access of different professions to junior positions might well correlate with new views and policies towards market–state relations. Beside this more fundamental reasoning, two rationales for change can be distinguished. First, a new ideology delivers different regulatory goals to be achieved (economic efficiency instead of securing the provision of a public commodity, for instance). Second, it claims that the same regulatory targets (e.g. economic efficiency) can be optimised by new mechanisms (i.e. regulatory modes). However, one would usually expect *not* to discover signs of regime failure – except 'crisis' and 'ideology' are both found to be forces driving regime change in the sector studied. It will be argued later that this holds, to some extent, for the regime 'revolution' in the telecommunications sector in the late 1980s and certainly for the emergence of a private broadcasting regime in the early 1980s.

Technological change

Most sectors of industry have undergone major technological changes. Technical innovations have not only had a direct impact on businesses, but sometimes pose a challenge to the incumbent regulatory regime (Dyson 1992a: 258). Again, two alternatives can be distinguished. First, they challenge incumbent regulatory modes by rendering them ineffective, e.g. the Internet. That means that old mechanisms do not work anymore or have sub-optimal results. Second, they challenge the incumbent regime, because desirable outcomes, which had formerly been technically impossible, are now within reach. Telecommunications represents an omnipresent example. This second alternative often goes hand in hand with a change of ideology regarding regulatory goals (see above). However, one would expect to identify co-relation between major technological innovations (such as satellite transmission of telephone calls or broadcasting signals) and some form of re-ordering of core market structures (such as new networks or access to the incumbent monopoly).

Globalisation

Globalisation is among the most debated issues of political and economic reasoning on the causes for change in a variety of fields in both political science, economics, international law and other disciplines. Unfortunately, the term is not used in a standardised form. In this study, globalisation should be understood as the growing together of formerly national or regional markets, accompanied by a higher intensity of international competition. This process is said to deprive national governments continuously of their power to govern the economy. Moreover, a certain trend in the market and in the development of market rules is assumed, ultimately leading towards a standardisation at the lowest level of market reglementation or restriction (*race to the bottom*). Correspondingly, where regime change is perceived as forced by globalisation (Dyson 1992: 5–7), one would expect to find a lowering of standards for and restrictions on market participants (especially supplier) as well as a convergence with the rules and standards of regimes of the same sector in other countries, i.e. the emergence of at least the basic elements of a global regime. Subscribing to international norms, or the ratification thereof, might be considered an observable implication. The regulation of banking in both Germany and the European Union since the 1980s is an outstanding example, especially with regard to regulatory modes and instruments.

Regionalisation (European integration)

Partly for historical reasons, and partly as a reaction to pressure from globalisation, a number of world regions strive for more intensified forms of co-operation. The European Union might be considered one of the most advanced organisations in terms of delegating authority to supra-national institutions. Legislative powers in significant areas have been transferred to the European Union, partly due to judicial activism by the European Court of Justice. In these areas, where national legislation is bound by a framework of ever more specific European law, national executive, legislative and partly judicial powers have considerably lost the inclination to govern certain sectors of industry (Dyson 1992a: 258). Nevertheless, both the depth and the width of European law still varies a lot cross-sectorally, due to the different legal bases, which EU institutions refer to when regulating these sectors. To identify different degrees of influence of EU law (there seems no doubt that there *is* such influence), one would expect the number of EU legal sources to indicate regulatory density (in terms of both depth (*intensity*) and width (*extent within the sector studied*)). That includes, of course, the scope of legislative authority in the respective field.

It can, however, not be denied *a priori* that EU institutions merely serve as an intervening variable with no substantial impact on their own regarding the regulation of sectors of industry. That is, EU institutions might be perceived as 'arenas' where member states can get their policies 'sanctioned' at the European level. Thus, in order to identify the degree of substantial impact of the European Union as a force driving regulatory change, one would have to compare proposals and demands by national governments, e.g. Germany, and the legislation passed at EU level. Vis-à-vis telecommunication regulation, it has been claimed by those in the know that EU developments have not been as important as they might look at first sight. However, even where EU institutions are mere 'arenas' for national interests, one could still assume that they are significant as 'catalysts', either speeding up national policy-making (which has been argued with regard to telecommunications re-regulation in Germany in the early 1990s), or spreading a national approach to other European member states, thereby strengthening national competitiveness.

Sub-national regionalisation and federalism

Federalism is a core element of the German polity. Legislative and executive powers are constitutionally granted either to the *Länder* or to the federal government. In some cases introduced into the German Basic Law in the 1960s, there are even shared authorities, but these do not play a part in the areas I have studied. Nevertheless, federalism does not only shape the organisational framework (especially with regard to *agency*) within which regulation takes place. As a variation of politics and the struggle for power, federalism can be a driving force for regulatory change, too. That is, where the *Länder* have specific interests, for instance, or where the federal government confronts possible losses of influence, the regulatory policies of the respective levels of government can be expected to become biased. The empirical findings of this study reveal that federalism and the significance of the institutional self-interest of *Länder* governments are evident in all sectors and can hardly be over-emphasised.

Policy-learning

Experiences of other governments abroad or of regulatory regimes in other sectors can provide useful information for creating or reforming regulation. Sometimes, they serve as a specimen to be 'imitated', sometimes they are conceived as a pool of ideas and possibilities one can choose from. Whether they serve for imitation or inspiration, gaining benefits from experiences in other countries or sectors qualifies as policy-learning not simply when there is a high degree of regulatory correspondence between regimes. Rather, one would expect to find specific and detailed references to the other regime. As will be seen later, in both cases of telecommunication and banking this rises to the level of importing complete terminologies without translating them into German.

Re-assessment on the part of the regulated

As mentioned above, *Capture Theory* suggests that regulation is a function, whose course depends on the demand for regulation by the regulated. Thus, regime *change* is assumed to correlate with a re-assessment of positions on regulatory policies on the part of the regulated. It should be noted, however, that the Capture Theory is designed rather to explain regulatory persistence than regime change (Noll and Owen 1983: 37–39). After all, regulation is said to benefit the regulated; so why change it? Only re-assessment by a considerable number of the regulated can provide an explanation that is still compatible with the basic thoughts in this line of argumentation. Hence, one would expect to find calls for reform from the regulated, published in order to prepare the public to accept what is being hammered out between regulators and the regulated behind the scenes. Furthermore, specific benefits for the regulated would have to be visible. The liberalisation of telecommunications in the 1980s represents a good example, where the interests of those directly or indirectly affected by the telecommunication regime have changed and hence support has increased for regime change.

This accumulation of topoi is, of course, not assumed to be complete. Similarly, it is not exclusive with regard to each other. In most cases, reality is too complex to allow for sufficient mono-causal explanations. By identifying different topoi as forces driving or enabling change and by weighing up their relative significance, I argue that we come as close to 'explaining' social realities as possible. However, this methodological question will be addressed in the following section. My sector-specific research has shown that by and large, this list of topoi included all major factors for regime development.

d) Case selection and methodology

After describing and explaining both the basic concepts of this study and the research design, it seems appropriate to add a few words on methodological issues as a conclusion for the theoretical part.

First of all, this study aims at contributing to both theoretical and empirical knowledge of the German political economy. The theory of the regulatory state is considered an analytical tool, much less a substantive explanation of statal or political change. It directs attention towards specific aspects of statehood in advanced industrial societies; aspects, which have always been there, but that have only recently gained special importance. The major theoretical problem thereby is that state-market relations are constructed in very different ways in Western industrial societies. Hence, a high level of abstraction is needed, so that international comparability can be achieved. This study does not claim to have developed *the* theory of the regulatory state, rather it has designed *one* possible approach usable in empirical research. In that sense, developing the regulatory state as an analytical concept is based on the more general rationale given by Ragin (1992a: 217–218):

> It is impossible to do research in a conceptual vacuum. Whether it is viewed as given or socially constructed, the empirical world is limitless in its detail, complexity, specificity, and uniqueness. The fact that we can make almost any every-day social category problematic (e.g. family, community, social class, church, firm, nation-state) is testimony to the complexity of the empirical. We make sense of its infinity by limiting it with our ideas. In effect, theoretical ideas and principles provide ways to see the empirical world and to structure our descriptions of this world.

In this sense, not abstraction but complexity is to be reduced, which shall be achieved with the concepts of both the regulatory state and regulatory regimes, including their sub-units. They support the first major heuristic goal of making temporal and cross-sectoral change (or variation) *observable.*

This book strives, however, to enlarge the empirical knowledge about the German political economy as well. It is designed to provide information, analysis and explanation of politico-economic (temporal) variations in specific sectors, yet it is not restricted to testing hypotheses, concerned with only an extremely limited scope of empirical reality, as advocated by Cook and Campbell (1979: 32), for instance. After all, the choice of research methods depends partly on this second heuristic goal, which means that maybe a less clear-cut, pure approach to identifying and explaining regulatory change has to be applied. This is why a rather large, open-ended list of topoi is used.

Here, a methodological problem appears. How can research on explaining regulatory change uncover parts of the conceptual tool kit it needs in order to know what it is looking for? That assertion incorporates legitimate criticism. In fact, in a Popperian view of doing (social as well as another) science this would not qualify as a sound design, in which there is a demand for verification and falsification of hypotheses, set up *a priori* to research (Popper 1959).

Such criticism shrinks down to the methodological problem of clarifying the relationship between dependent variable, independent variable(s) and the selection of cases. After all, as argued by Becker (1992: 205), it translates into the 'problem of what we can say about what we've found out in our research'.

First of all, as advocated by Abbott (1983) and others, scientific discovery can focus on the dependent variable to be explained as a historical *process*. That is, the thing to be explained is assumed to have come about through a series of steps and not as something that has happened all at once. As Becker (1992: 209) has summarised:

> The analysis focuses first on discovering the sequence of steps involved in the process under study. The causal analysis takes the form of a tree diagram, showing how a case progresses from step to step in the *story*, each step understood as preceding in time the one that follows it. The *treelike character* of the analysis is not simply a useful visual convention. The analyst intends it to mirror how the result has 'really' come about. The *process* is taken to be important to the result, perhaps even *constitutive* of it .... Instead of an outcome described as a value of a variable (so many steps up in a hierarchy, so much more or less income), the outcome is described as a different form of organizational or individual activity, a different way of putting together a number of common and interdependent activities. (author's italics)

In other words, discovering what exactly the end result – the *dependent* variable – is, becomes at least one major object of research, which explains why this approach has been labelled as *narrative analysis* (Becker 1992: 208–209). 'Analysis of the dependent variable' (Paul Lazarsfeld) is intended as an important part of the research endeavour. This might seem to some as delivering explanations that are tautological, yet not in a formal-logical sense, but understood as the 'statement of a sequence (of steps, (author)) in which is prefigured ... the end result' (Becker 1992: 210). However, clarifying what the dependent variable is – in the course of research (!) – is possible, at least if one treats it as an object that has an inherent temporal component. According to this assumption, *only* the conduct of analyses and research on the phenomenon studied can reveal all factors that contribute to its coming into existence. Otherwise, even the phenomenon itself cannot really be understood. In that sense, differentiating between dependent and independent variables becomes almost obsolete; after all, independent variables are somehow conceived as the constitutive elements of the dependent variable.

Nevertheless, this work does not fully subscribe to such reasoning. Even though I agree that a complete understanding of social phenomena usually requires a historical perspective, including knowledge of the 'sequence of steps' that have preceded its appearance, political science strives for more than a full account of things that have happened. It aims to find some kind of principle that governs how things come about. It searches for conditions, rules and ideally for 'laws', which represent a generalisation of the ways social phenomena arise, develop, and disappear (also Gellner 1985: 89). That is what Zuckerman (1991: 1) means, when he summarises:

> When we do political science, we set out to discover uniformities in the political world. We assume that the swirl of political events ... can be understood in rather simple and precise ways. We develop concepts, hypotheses, and theories in order to describe and explain politics .... Political science, like any science, uses analytical techniques to posit and explore regularities in the world around us.

That is, political science analysis reaches beyond the specifics of a case (Brown 1987: vi), even though it sometimes implies a harsh reduction of complexity and interconnections. It also intends to say something about the cases *not* studied. That is why a balance has to be found between the full historical account of cases on the one hand and extreme generalisation (focusing on the smallest possible number of explanatory factors) on the other.

This study aims to find that balance, firstly, by using a rather abstract conceptualisation of the dependent variable (i.e. the regulatory state), second, an amendable series of explanatory topoi (which in Abbott's approach are constitutive of the dependent variable; hence, there should be room for expansion left over) and third, a broad selection of cases, so that via categorisation of types of goals, institutions and modes, (and the same holds for the topoi) abstraction and substantial theory-building about the change of the regulatory state, and ultimately statehood, is, at least to some extent, possible.

Even though the design of this work is inspired by King, Keohane and Verba's (1994) most important contribution, it cannot apply their approach of looking for causal relationship. There is nothing wrong with such an approach – as argued above, it is necessary to eventually come up with respective hypotheses in order to generalise – but at this early stage of research on regulation in Germany, something else is needed for methodology. In fact, King, Keohane and Verba (1994: 36–41) themselves have labelled what is done here as *thick description*. This means that I shall try to trace pathways between the set of 'independent variables', or as I prefer *topoi*, and the dependent variable, i.e. sector-specific change of the regulatory state. It is impossible at this stage, to generate strong hypotheses on one or two independent variables and to choose cases on these variables instead of other criteria, as has been done here. This study is designed to provide some groundwork for further research, that will then be able to look for causal relationship.

The concept of topoi dates back to the art of rhetoric in classic Greece and Rome. Originally designed to help the speaker find arguments and furthermore, consider all important aspects of a given theme, it has found its way into science, especially into jurisprudence. There are three major advantages of an approach using topoi instead of a fixed set of (testable, conventional) hypotheses. First, as theory is not an end in itself, neither is testing theories. Thus, theories whose degree of generalisation and (what seems even more troublesome) simplification is extremely high, run the risk of contributing too little to the understanding of the cases studied. This is, however, one major objective of this work. Hence, even though I intend to further the development of theory, the latter aim has to be counterbalanced against the first. Second, an amendable list of possible causes (including the specification of expected observations, which has been provided above) is open for 'discovery by chance' (*Zufallsfunde*). This work is not intended to be the ultimate end product of research. Rather, it intends to uncover the process of scientific discovery, including at least most of the considerations that come up during the course of research. In that sense, I shall strive for a didactic presentation of results, i.e. also uncovering the reasoning which has not been proved to be empirically tenable. Third, topoi seem to be, as surprising as it might sound, analytically and methodologically superior to the testing of fixed hypotheses. This is so, because it cannot be ruled out that similar observations (in two or more cases) have quite different causes, due to both multi-causality *and* multiple causalities. With regard to the first (multi-causality), it is a well-established proposition of social science methodology that causal variables are not really independent (Becker 1992: 208). Rather, as analysed by Ragin (1987), they are effective (only) when they operate in concert. However, this kind of conjunctural influence of variables neither implies that the variables, which have to be present for a particular outcome to occur, have the same importance, nor that their relative importance is fixed. That is what multiple causality attempts to grasp: even where similar outcomes occur, the relative impact of factors has to be re-assessed. The concept of topoi seems to facilitate this, because the approach is less likely to forget about empirical details in the light of apparently consistent test results.

However, using a tripartite set of possible causes for regime change could have been an alternative: *public interest approach*, *interest group approach*, and *public choice approach* (Francis 1993: 7–9). This categorisation, as described earlier, focuses on *actors* as sources of change. The public interest approach assumes *the state* to be both an independent and a self-reliant actor, pursuing its own goals and strategies. Second, the interest group approach displays *societal groups* a as causing factor for change. Here, the state is either conceived as an 'arena' for interest group politics (*pluralist perspective*) or a partner somehow integrating these groups (*corporatist perspective*). Finally, the public choice approach concentrates on the *individual* (mostly located in regulatory institutions), perceived as rational and profit maximising, as the driving force in regulatory politics.

Even though such a tripartite system of potential sources for regulatory change has its merits, one major methodological problem remains. After all, it is always the regulatory state, which has to decide upon regulatory policies. Thus, whenever a specific policy cannot be clearly traced back to either interest group influence or individual striving for career promotion, it will be identified as the politically 'neutral' outcome, defined by the independent, self-reliant state. Such reasoning *ex negativo* seems inevitable in a system, where the ultimate decision-making unit (the state) is also conceived as one potential source for policy-making.

The *case selection* has already been explained with regard to its significance for the regulatory state. The cases chosen represent the 'most different cases' with regard to the levels of government involved, the relationship between public and private enterprise, the legacy of state interference into private activities and the incumbent regime at the turn of the millennium. Methodological problems of 'casing', as brought up by Ragin (1992) and many others, do not seem to play a major role here. *Case* does, however, refer in this study only to the fields of regulation studied, understood as 'contrasting event sequences' (Ragin 1992a: 5). The possible conflation with 'causes', 'variables' (Ragin 1992a) and the like are hopefully settled and hence excluded.

RegTP cannot do without 'single permits' (*Einzelgenehmigungen*) and therefore had to find ways to assess and determine 'efficient cost of service'. The respective decree (TEntgV) provides not only for the legal norm to base decisions on information from the regulated and their accounting systems (because they are insufficient and not necessarily reliable), but also for the so-called 'comparative markets procedure' (*Vergleichsmarktverfahren*). The latter is based on the assumption that there are comparable markets (either domestic or international) which may serve as a yardstick to determine what 'efficient cost of service' is. The procedure has already been applied by the regulator, but was challenged before the courts (Geppert *et al.* 1998: 308-18). One of the reasons for the lawsuit is certainly that transparency of country selection was not given. In fact, it seems that the regulator had considerable discretion here, which, as mentioned on several occasions, violates to some extent the rule-of-law doctrine, as traditionally understood by German administrations.

Even though formally *ex ante* regulation is the more 'severe' regulatory instrument, *ex post* regulation can be more painful for both the regulated and also the consumers. It does not only concern those prices not covered by *ex ante* regulation, but ultimately all. This is so, because § 30 TKG gives RegTP the right to interfere in those cases, where it learns about discriminatory practices or anti-competitive price reductions – no matter whether the price in question had originally been permitted by the regulator or not. After checking in detail, RegTP can order the regulated company to change fees accordingly. Such decisions are publicised. Making prices subject to *de facto* 'permanent' (potential) control by RegTP shows the enormous importance of proactive interference of the regulator to establish a working, competitive market order. It is *not* a matter of consumer-oriented price policy-making, i.e. guaranteeing low telecommunication fees. This is best illustrated by an early decision of the regulator concerning directory inquiries of DTAG. A competitor had filed a complaint to the former ministry that DTAG charges unfairly low fees for its helpline. BMPT ordered DTAG to raise fees in accordance with the principle of efficient cost of service, i.e. without cross-subsidisation, and the price then rose from DM 0.60 to DM 1.92 per minute. However, it has also been argued that the regulator displays a certain tendency to make compromises and is inconsistent to some extent about strict enforcement of a pro-competitive price order (Geppert *et al.* 1998: 210).

Finally, as *price regulation* is understood here as the core element of regulation of market behaviour, we need to turn quickly to a complementary part, i.e. the regulation of the general terms of business (*Allgemeine Geschäftsbedingungen (AGB)*). While price regulation is the quantitative side of regulating market behaviour, regulation of AGBs is the qualitative one. Only when combined do price and AGBs determine what services really 'are' for consumers/purchasers. AGB regulation is, in short, first and foremost a *consumer protection regulation*. Just like price regulation, consumer protection is organised asymmetrically, i.e. market-dominant companies (e.g. DTAG) are subject to more severe control by the regulator than competitors. Beyond that, while the duties of market-dominant suppliers differ from those of all others (§§ 2-33 TKV), consumer rights are designed symmetrically (§ 97 TKG).

Nevertheless, AGBs are subject to *ex ante* approval by the regulator (§ 23 TKG) and this duty extends to all market participants symmetrically. Characteristics of AGB regulation are fundamentally defined by EU law, which had been transformed into domestic law by the 1998 version of the relevant decree (TKV). Although primarily directed towards consumer protection, AGB regulation is also influenced by the general principle of proactive creation of a competitive market order. The latter concerns discriminatory practices of market-dominant suppliers with regard to competitors demanding certain services. This exemplifies the general approach of the *Postreform III* regime – as far as its compliance aspects are concerned – to treat (private) consumers and competing companies purchasing services from the incumbent, market-dominant DTAG equally.

In short, price regulation is relatively hierarchical, 'old fashioned' and harsh, just like the regulation for entry into the market. Especially with regard to the market-dominant DTAG, the TKG seems to have little trust in DTAG's willingness to play fairly. As will be seen later, practice has shown that this assumption was not completely wrong. However, elements of 'responsive regulation' (Ayres and Braithwaite 1995) are incorporated by allowing the regulated to go along with a range of other charges in the first place and RegTP to come in with regulatory sanctions only *ex post*. Furthermore the new regime has opted for the more innovate *price cap* regulation as the primary mechanism to control price variations. Taken together with the fact, that for the remaining cases of a modified form of *rate of return* regulation, based on single-case decisions, the 'comparative market procedure' (assessing prices in other, comparable markets abroad) has been set up as an alternative to evaluate more or less sound internal accounting material of the regulated, we can therefore conclude that the *Postreform III* regime was able to learn from foreign experience or to let other nation's practices have an effect when deciding future cases. It should also be mentioned here that RegTP refers to a closely related think tank, the *WIK*, when it comes to details of price regulation (as well as other aspects of regulatory instruments applied). WIK is staffed with research experts and hence provides for a 'gateway' from the 'epistemic community' to influence regulatory policies[8].

Third-party access (Open Network Access and Interconnection)

Access to the incumbent network of DTAG is particularly crucial for competitors in the telecommunication market. The law governing third-party access is largely based on EU Directives and a range of subsequent recommendations. It is based on three regulatory goals in particular: first, providing for open, efficient and equal access to public telecommunications networks and services; second, ensuring fair competition; and third, the harmonisation of technical prerequisites for network access and interconnection as well as framework conditions for pricing necessary to enable all market participants to make use of their rights to access other telecommunication networks. As telecommunications is an extremely dynamic market, the EU Commission is supported by the so-called 'ONP-committee', which comprises representatives from the member states and the Commission, to prepare future legal action by the EU Commission (Art. 9 I 90/387/EEC).

The regulation of network access is at the heart of RegTP's activities to proactively support the emergence of a working market order in the telecommunication sector. It implies a plethora of different regulatory activities from price and condition issues to technical specifics, all of which are intrinsically interrelated with major, sometimes unforeseeable implications for the future of telecommunication business development. Before we turn to highlight the core elements and mechanisms of network access regulation as set up by the TKG, I must emphasise what lies at the bottom of the problems exposed here. Third-party access as a doctrine to establish a market order is effectively a means, stemming from general competition policy, of restricting the network owner's property rights. The latter has no interest in giving competitors access to the very basis of his business, especially when the incumbent used to serve the whole community as a monopoly. On the other hand, building complete networks for both long-distance connections as well as the local loop is extremely costly and time-consuming. With regard to connecting single households (local loop), it is even questionable, to what extent parallel networks make sense. 'Wireless local loop' technologies, such as DECT or CDMA, may to some extent be a substitute for wires, but they are certainly no way out of the general problem. This is made even more complicated by the fact that new marketeers will construct lucrative long-distance connections first, including specific lines to important consumers, such as major companies. The local loop represents an investment of secondary importance due to the high costs, limited profit margins and long-term planning. In short, as well as the 'property rights' argument there is also a 'cream skimming' problem at stake here, both of which have to be carefully balanced against the necessary regulatory restrictions for the incumbent, former monopoly to enable liberalisation to become effective.

Three core elements of third-party access can be distinguished. First, 'special network access' (*besonderer Netzzugang*), which must allow for competitors to use the incumbent's complete network to generate a viable and sustainable service programme to be offered on the market. Second, 'interconnection', which is a special form of the above and refers to inter-operability of different networks in order to make sure that users can build up telephone connections with each other. Third, 're-sale', which means a form of competition *on* existing networks without substantially bringing in new capacity. The latter equals 're-billing', as re-sellers buy network capacities and re-sell them 'piece by piece' to their customers, effectively creating arbitrage profits (i.e. the difference between the 'wholesale' price they pay to the network operator and the fees they charge to their clients). Two further aspects are to be mentioned with regard to 're-sale'. First, there is a general duty of all market participants to permit re-sale on their networks, a provision which has been criticised for both legal and economic reasons (Geppert *et al.* 1998: 226). Here, the rationale of liberalisation and creating new areas for competition has almost fully displaced other concerns, including not only property rights, but also new network operating companies' interest in preserving a certain 'exclusion zone' to develop a standing in the market. Second, RegTP has not been provided with a price rule (§ 9 TKV); only the general prohibition of discrimination. In Germany there is a certain 'regulatory deficit' as opposed to the United States, where there is a rule for fixing the prices and where the very idea of 're-selling' comes from. Moreover, a chance was lost by not legally granting those re-sellers, who contribute to network infrastructure by building networks on their own, a certain price advantage.

However, 'special network access' and 'interconnection' represent the core elements most problematic to the regulatory business of RegTP. The law provides for different degrees of regulatory interference with regard to the means employed by the regulator. While network access is subject to asymmetrical regulation, i.e. only market-dominant network operators are coerced by law to enable competitors to access their network (§ 35 TKG), interconnection is subject to symmetrical regulation, i.e. every network operator must offer network interconnection *on demand* (§§ 36-7 TKG). Similarly, in case of unsuccessful negotiations between network operators, the enforcement mechanisms to be employed by RegTP must be identified. While network access regulation contains (only) § 33 TKG 'observance of misuse' authority (*Mißbrauchsaufsicht*), interconnection regulation includes the power of RegTP to hierarchically command interconnection (*Zusammenschaltungsanordnung*), including fundamental trading terms (§ 37 TKG). However, it must be emphasised that in both cases a voluntarily negotiated solution (*Verhandlungslösung*), found by both parties, is given priority; RegTP action is always secondary. In the case of a specific demand for network access, both parties can ask for 'arbitration proceedings' (*Schlichtungsverfahren*), which remains, however, on a voluntary basis (§ 8 NZV). Table 4.5 summarises the 'pyramidal' enforcement mechanisms of both network access and interconnection regulation.

Table 4.5: Stages of enforcement mechanisms employed by RegTP

	(Special) Network Access (*besonderer Netzzugang*)	Interconnection (*Zusammenschaltung*)
Stage 3 or alternative to Stage 2	Observance of misuse procedure (*Mißbrauchsaufsicht*)	
Stage 2	Arbitration proceedings (*Schlichtungsverfahren*)	Order of interconnection (*Zusammenschaltungsan-ord-nung*)
Failure of Stage 1	Appeal to regulator by both parties	Appeal to regulator by one or both parties
Stage 1	Negotiation (duty of mar-ket-dominant network operator)	Negotiation (duty of all network operators on demand)

Table 4.5 makes clear that the ultimate sanctions employed by RegTP do not necessarily differ with regard to severity (ultimately, RegTP can in both cases enforce compliance with the legally intended access and/or interconnection to/of networks by hierarchical means), but vis-à-vis the logic of initiating the next step. And this has implications for the time-frame, within which enforcement on behalf of the regulator can take place. Put in other words, the 'responsiveness' to the behaviour of the regulated is not homogeneously transformed by regulatory modes.

If we look for the rationale for different compliance 'pyramids', we have to take into account what has been outlined above: the introduction of ways and means for competitors to build up their business by using DTAG infrastructure substantially infringes on the latter's property rights, not to mention the likely (and politically intended) loss of market shares to new marketeers. Despite the obvious, general primacy of liberalisation, the practical transformation of modes to ensure a certain degree of DTAG co-operation (with the competitors demanding network access) requires a more careful approach for both constitutional, legal and strategic reasons. After all, 'mandated compliance' is the least feasible option for regulators, as this will lead to both a range of practical inefficiencies between the incumbent ex-monopoly and competitors as well as numerous litigation cases. The latter keep regulatory work of RegTP under a constant proviso of a final judicial decision of the court, making it extremely hard for the regulator to build up a certain standing and a reliable, predictable and sustainable regulatory approach. That seems to me a major reason for providing the option of arbitration proceedings, conducted in the 'decision-taking chamber' procedure (*Beschlußkammerverfahren*), very similar to the way in which judicial assessment works in court (§ 73 TKG).

This said, German 'judicialism' prevails even here. There have already been a series of litigation cases involving DTAG. It is impossible to reproduce the whole process of building up the case law, but two major cases will be identified to exemplify typical problems of the regulatory modes set up by the law. They are almost paradigmatic as they illustrate the kinds of rationales and interests driving both DTAG and competitors when dealing with each other and the regulator. However, it seems worthwhile mentioning here that RegTP has not lost one of the 400 cases that have been pursued in the first two years following its creation.

The first case involves one of the three principles set up by NZV regarding the duties of market-dominant network operators when offering network access to competitors:[9] *unbundling*. DTAG intended to force its competitors (Mannesmann Arcor, NetCologne and o.tel.o), who demanded network access, to use a certain transmission technology, which is not absolutely necessary for the use of DTAG infrastructure. In a first decision in 1997, the regulator (the former ministry) decided in favour of the competitors. The administrative court in Cologne, to which DTAG appealed, came to a similar conclusion, but held that DTAG could not be expected to re-construct its infrastructure according to the demands of competitors. However, while this was technically not necessary here, the court found that beyond this proviso, the goal of fostering competition in the telecommunication market, as prescribed in the TKG, must be given priority over property rights and other management interests of DTAG (VG Köln AZ 1 L 2317/97). Before the court of appeal in Münster took a formal decision, it declared that it was more in favour of the arguments put forward by the competitors. As a consequence, DTAG put forward another offer, closer to what the competitors wanted. In February 2000, the court of appeal decided accordingly and thereby confirmed RegTP's decision (OVG Münster AZ 13 A 179/99 and AZ 13A 180/99).

The case illustrates that network access is *still* essentially a legal-technical-economic problem, combining property rights arguments with the creation of a liberalised, market order of telecommunications and technical feasibility. The balance to be found is dynamic, and even where the regulator – despite its institutional 'legacy' as successor to part of the BMPF-DBP-complex – had taken a courageous decision in favour of competition, it is up to the courts to point to the kind of 'balance' we will experience in practice.

The second case to be illustrated here involves the regulation of access charges. Remuneration for network access (*Netzzugangsentgelte*) is subject to a special form of price regulation (§ 39 TKG), based either on the usual 'rate of return' or 'price cap' approach, the latter being restricted by § 7 II TEntgV. What is different compared to 'normal' price regulation is, however, that, for instance, after determining the 'efficient cost of service', certain components, which do not directly apply to the kind of service demanded, are to be deducted. In effect, 'unbundling' leads to certain cost advantages for competitors demanding access.

To allow for easier contracting between DTAG and competitors demanding network access, § 6 V NZV empowers the regulator to lay down a so-called 'basic offer' (*Grundangebot*) after DTAG has successfully negotiated with competitors and found agreement. This basic offer contains conditions concerning network access of a more general nature, which are expected to be used in future agreements. In practice, RegTP will probably base such a basic offer on what had been negotiated before. Obviously, this legal norm is designed according to the so-called 'standard interconnection offer' (*Standardzusammenschaltungsangebot*) as mandated by EU Directive 97/33/EG. According to the latter, market-dominant network operators (such as DTAG) must issue *ex ante* a standard contract, containing the conditions under which any access-demanding competitor will be allowed to interconnect its network to DTAG's. However, the 'basic offer' and the 'standard interconnection offer' differ in two aspects. First, while the first is laid down by the regulator, the latter has to be issued by the regulated. And second, while the first is publicised *ex post*, the second must be made public *ex ante*. Despite a 'specimen contract' (*Mustervereinbarung*) issued by DTAG in 1997, it was questionable whether it complied with EU law requirements. After all, in the October 1997 report of the EU Commission vis-à-vis transformation of EU liberalisation norms in the telecommunication sector this lack of a DTAG standard interconnection offer was a central point of critique. Nevertheless, the Commission later accepted the 'specimen contract' and the issue has since been dismissed.

In the first relevant case in 1997 concerning access charges, DTAG tried to include everything which had some relation to the demands made in the interconnection of its network with those of Mannesmann Arcor and o.tel.o, including past burdens (*Beiträge zur Abdeckung von Altlasten*). Determining what the service is when interconnection is demanded is certainly a special problem, because the question arises, whether historical developments leading to the incumbent network as operated by DTAG today (such as massive, expensive investments in the former GDR or higher prices for facilities, due to fostering German producers before liberalisation) are an integral part of the service to be bought by the competitor demanding access. In the case at stake, the former regulator (BMPT) applied the above-mentioned 'comparative market procedure'

(*Vergleichsmarktverfahren*) but put a time limit on its decision. The reason for the latter is that DTAG's internal accounting documents had been useless for regulatory purposes at that time, but that they should in the future form the basis for interconnection prices (Geppert *et al.* 1998: 308-18). It was also hoped that the EU Commission would pass more detailed regulation regarding components and methods suitable to determine the appropriate interconnection price (It did later so by passing directive 97/33/EC, appendix II). However, what must be concluded from the above is, first, regulation of interconnection and the actual conditions (including prices) connected with it must probably be considered an area of intensive regulatory activity on behalf of the regulator. Solutions found in negotiations, which DTAG will always be a part of in the foreseeable future, seem rather exceptional. Second, the interconnection of networks involves highly detailed problems of cost accounting systems and cost classification, demanding expert knowledge of the regulator. And third, if the TKG's variation of 'rate of return' regulation, i.e. efficient cost of service regulation, is to be practised successfully, it implies a standardisation of cost accounting, especially with regard to DTAG. In other words, there is still need for further regulation. The interesting aspect of the latter is that although accounting procedures seem somewhat removed from the regulatory business of RegTP, it turns out that they represent a necessary prerequisite for price control.

Finally, it should be mentioned that learning from foreign experience has not given the full picture. While there is some general, international convergence with regard to the costs to be taken into account when determining the appropriate price for network access (or interconnection), and moreover, imitation of legal-technical figures from the American model, such as the so-called *essential facilities* doctrine (Engel and Knieps 1998), there are still major differences with regard to institutional and procedural solutions. Some of these might serve as models for Germany, e.g. the detailed determination of what can be unbundled (and must be unbundled on demand) in the United States.

Universal service

Providing a universal service is a social duty, referring to *equality*-rationales. As mandated by Art. 87 f of the Basic Law, the federal government has a duty to provide for a nation-wide telecommunication infrastructure, even though it may not produce and/or maintain this infrastructure by itself. In that sense, state control of infrastructure requirements and universal service in particular is a prototype case of 'regulation', because the state as regulator has no service-generating function, but makes private actors do their business in a way compatible with a politically (here, also constitutionally) pre-defined public interest. The question, which arises from the above is therefore, 'who' shall provide 'how much' universal service, paid by 'whom'? There are several models suggesting different answers to this tripartite set of questions. Once more, a balance has to be found: on the one hand, *cream skimming* must be prevented – which implies that all competitors should be called on to contribute substantially to a country-wide infrastructure, including even the less attractive investments. On the other hand, imposing costly investment requirements on newcomers all too early might hamper their business development, ultimately endangering the liberalisation project as a whole.

The system of universal service regulation set up in Germany answers the three questions above as follows. First, the definition of what 'universal service' is and shall contain is *not* included in the TKG, but left to the respective decree (TUDLV). The latter was passed by the *Bundesregierung* with *Bundesrat* approval, according to the formal requirements of § 17 II TKG, after intensive debate with the *Länder* concerning the scope of universal service. The very rule of decision-making on these fundamental aspects of universal service illustrates that all the political actors had been extremely aware of the crucial importance of sufficient telecommunication services in all regions. The *Länder* must be seen as 'watchdogs', concerned about relative advantages and disadvantages of their less-developed regions. It is hardly surprising that the definition passed in 1997 is more extensive, compatible with the EU definition if not similar and, for example, includes ISDN characteristics of telephone connections.

A rather strict definition of what 'reasonable prices' (*Erschwinglichkeit*) means, as mandated by the TKG, is also found in the decree. § 2 TUDLV determines the 'reasonable price' in detail for different elements of universal service, including a reference to the prices paid by private households in areas outside cities in 1997. Generally speaking, regulations vis-à-vis price control of universal service seem to either grant the status quo a certain normative power, or refer explicitly to other, established forms of telecommunication price regulation, such as TEntgV's variation of the 'rate of return' approach (Klodt *et al.* 1995: 176).

Even though the *Postreform III* regime, as opposed to all of its predecessors, assumes that a competitive market order in the telecommunication sector is generally able to provide for universal service, the law includes norms and rules for cases of 'market failure', which, as such, qualify as a form of extremely *strong regulation.* First, according to § 9 I (1) TKV, customers are given a subjective, legal right to receive universal service from the company, which is obliged to provide such services. That means in turn, that as well as RegTP's checking of sufficient delivery of universal service, consumers themselves are entitled to litigation and other legal action to ensure their sufficient supply with telecommunication services.

Second, and this is the more important element, procedures to deal with a regional or material lack of a universal service supply are strictly determined by law, generating costs of different kinds on behalf of the regulated competitors in the market. This universal service regime contains in essence the following features. First, it is up to RegTP to decide whether there is a lack of supply anywhere of universal service (§ 19 I TKG). Second, all licensed competitors in the relevant material and regional market, with a market share of 4 per cent or more (calculated on the basis of the national market) – or fulfilling the criteria of market-dominance according to general competition law (§ 22 GWB) – are obliged to contribute to supplying universal service, be it by factually supplying the services demanded or be it by financially contributing to the costs (§ 18 I TKG). If no supplier is willing to do the job, RegTP will check which market-dominant competitors are active on the relevant market (§ 19 II and III TKG). The following steps depend on the number of potential suppliers (none, one or several) and whether they demand compensation for universal service supply or not (§ 19 TKG). RegTP can oblige any or several of these candidates to provide for universal service in the relevant market without compensation. With regard to selecting the future provider of universal services, RegTP has considerable discretion, limited only by the non-discrimination principle.

Third, a new set of options opens up when one, or several, of the candidates is/are obliged by RegTP to show satisfactorily that it/they is/are entitled to financial compensation (§ 19 IV TKG), i.e. convincing the regulator that long-running incremental costs, including a fair profit, caused by the provision of a universal service in the relevant market, will exceed foreseeable returns (§ 20 TKG, § 2 TUDLV)). The cost accounting procedure here is crucial, because it substantially forms the basis of what the respective provider would get as financial compensation, if RegTP decides to maintain its obligation. In the latter case, the obliged provider will receive compensation *ex post*, so RegTP can check whether returns were actually lower than costs. Nevertheless, as the calculation of the compensation is not based on factual costs, but on the 'efficient cost of service', the actual compensation at the end of each year still remains somehow far from what the accounting sheet testifies.

However, after receiving these calculations, RegTP *may* call for tenders (*Ausschreibungsverfahren*). Here, all companies are invited to participate and submit their bids. RegTP will choose not only on the basis of the lowest compensation demanded, but also take into account expertise and reliability of the bidders. Contrary to the procedure above, RegTP's choice of one of the bids determines the compensation granted (§§ 19 V and 20 III TKG). The regime merely assumes that the result of a competitive call for tenders will be that bidders calculate very tight prices. But a range of scenarios are imaginable, where this 'hope for efficiency' might be disappointed. Whether the lack of a correction mechanism will prove to be a regulatory shortfall, must be left to the future regulatory practice.

Fourth, the costs for financial compensation have to be borne by market-dominant service suppliers (the so-called 'universal service contribution' (*Universaldienstabgabe*)) made by those with a market share of 4 per cent or more of the relevant market as related to the national market (§§ 21 and 22 TKG). Consequently, the community of service providers of a specific market is liable for ensuring a reliable universal service – at least financially. The latter has been a major point of criticism (e.g. Schwintowski 1997: 632-3).

If we now look at the causes of this universal service regime, it seems hard to find conclusive answers. The system as presented above is rather unique in an advanced industrial society and has no model. Moreover, beyond the definition of what universal service is and which quality parameters are to be applied, the German regime is substantially incompatible with the range of options defined by the EU (Geppert *et al.* 1998: 367-74). The fact that there is no experience available, turns such a complex system into an experiment. One wonders, why legislators, otherwise always open to policy-learning from abroad, have neither opted for the American bond system, administered by a Federal-State Joint Board, or the reformed British 'pay or play' regime, established in 1997, or finally the French 'surplus charge' approach. What distinguishes the German regime from these is, among many details, that on the one hand, it leaves an amazingly high degree of discretion with the regulator (at least up to the point, where RegTP decides to call for tenders), and on the other hand, it guarantees to some extent that new market competitors are not bound to *technically* contribute to the provision of universal service. That the latter are, however, not fully released from responsibility might be attributed to the fact that the anti-liberalisation coalition (inside and outside parliament) demanded that all market suppliers should be subject to the duty of providing universal service. This must be seen in the context of the discussion on whether licences should be issued only on a nation-wide basis (i.e. all licensed competitors would have to serve the whole market of the country) or whether regionally limited licences should be included. While the latter prevailed, a compromise was made to give those serving the national market certain prerogatives with regard to assignment of scarce resources (particularly frequencies). And all suppliers are potentially integrated into the community of those subject to the universal service obligation (Voeth 1996: 178-87).

Here, it becomes obvious what has been reported by RegTP officials: the whole regime governing universal service is primarily a symbolic act to accommodate the worries of the parliamentary opposition that a fully liberalised telecommunication sector might eventually lead to a 'retreat' from less profitable areas (or customers). However, as far as those are concerned who prepared the bill, there was never any intention to include such a regime in the new law. The original planning did not consider a universal service regime necessary in

Germany. Therefore, the main rationale for the regime now incumbent was to make it the least intrusive as possible, i.e. the least costly for newcomers in the market. If viewed from that perspective, the regime makes a lot of sense, as it causes no immediate costs on behalf of market suppliers in the first place. However, a universal service provision has positive regulatory effects, too. As for DTAG's plans to reduce the number of public telephones in German cities, the potential threat of intervention by the regulator has caused the former monopolist to negotiate with local governments about alternatives.

Technicalities

Beyond the core regulatory functions, RegTP is concerned with the more technical tasks of telecommunication regulation, which account for about 80 per cent of RegTP's day-to-day work. They involve only partially re-distributive or allocative implications; instead, administration of telephone numbers or frequencies, telecommunication security, including licensing of new facilities, is usually a rather unspectacular business. However, it results in complex decision-making situations, involving physical, technical, international and, of course, also politico-economic aspects. Among the many points I could raise here, three will be dealt with. First, the regulator has, in accordance with the law (§§ 59-63 TKG), delegated some of its tasks to private or semi-private institutions. A well-established procedure of 'accrediting' such institutions to fulfil public functions (*hoheitliche Aufgaben*) has a long tradition in Germany. The routine inspections of cars to ensure their technical safety by the *Technische Überwachungsvereine* (TÜV) is familiar to all German car drivers. Similarly, the TKG grants TÜV and others certain authority regarding safety inspections of facilities etc. Second, as telecommunications raises questions of data safety or interception and bugging, another federal institution, the 'commissioner for data protection' (*Bundesbeauftragter für Datenschutz*) is involved (§ 91 TKG). He monitors illegal practices with regard to the above and informs RegTP if legal or other action is required. In any case, regulatory power and discretion has been left with the regulator. Third, and this follows from the above, RegTP has complete jurisdiction vis-à-vis enforcement. The latter includes quasi-state attorney power to inquire, to seize documents or to examine witnesses.

e) Summary and evaluation

Looked upon in retrospect, the three *Postreforms* of 1989, 1994 and 1996 seem to form a logical series. *Postreform I* and *II* appear to be seminal steps towards the completion of the liberalisation project in *Postreform III*. However, as a closer look at the content of the reforms, and, moreover, the causes for their implementation shows, it seems more than doubtful that decision-makers in the mid and late 1980s were aware of what their initial reform project would eventually become.

The above sections have already summarised key features of the regulatory regime in the telecommunication sector. Table 4.6 attempts, however, to put the findings in a nutshell.

Table 4.6: *Legitimacy*, *agency* and *compliance* in telecommunications

	Old Regime	***Postreform I* regime**	***Postreform II* regime**	***Postreform III* regime**
Legitimacy	Equality	Equality, partly efficiency	Equality and efficiency	Efficiency and equality
Agency	Regulator–regulated complex; politicisation of institutional arrangement; hierarchical organisation; considerable influence of the *Länder*	As above; 're-branding' strategy; limited institutional change according to the needs of a partly liberalised market	Institutional separation of regulator and regulated (now formally and partly also materially privatised) monopoly; organisational innovations; increased influence of the *Länder* as compensatory reaction	Complete separation and de-politicisation of regulator; strong reduction of institution-alised *Länder* influence
Compliance	Compulsory, hierarchical orders (public (administrative) law))	As above.; traditional rather restrictive regulatory means (licensing etc.)	Transitory phase: starting loss of hierarchical (administrative-legal) means while underdeveloped availability of regulatory ones	Traditional as well as innovative regulatory means; asymmetrical approach

One could certainly understand the three *Postreform* stages as serving different purposes. While *Postreform I* aimed at the liberalisation of the 'new' telecommunication sub-markets as well as the non-sensitive areas (e.g. facilities), *Postreform II* was about strengthening Telekom's international competitiveness. Only *Postreform III* finally intended to introduce a competitive market regime.

It is difficult to summarise answers to the question what accounts for regulatory change in telecommunications, not only because several forces had been at work – multi-causality is, as mentioned earlier, something every serious student of regulatory change would expect anyway – but also due to the very nature of 'procedural reform', whose final regime is to be seen as the last step in a series of different stages. Initially, the first reform efforts of 1989 had to confront both a strong anti-change coalition network, stretching beyond DBP and the ministry, and also constitutional hurdles. This network acted as a 'rent-seeking coalition', providing for a stable consensus among DBP, dependent suppliers and the ministry, which, according to the organisational logic of self-preservation, had certainly no interest in reform towards liberalisation. However, as the problems of collective action had diminished on behalf of DBP customers, because suppliers realised the potential of new markets at the end of the 1970s, a 'structural window' opened for politics to come in and start the reform. In that sense, theories on un-governability were definitely proven wrong by reality.

While a distinct, yet not extremely progressive *regulatory ideology*, as manifested by a government white paper in 1984, provided for the necessary stimulus, the very process of formulating a reform programme displayed a high degree of consent-orientation. *Federalism* in particular played a role in the second reform step of 1994, because here the constitutional foundations for the latter market regime were laid. However, the *Länder* were certainly no force for change, rather their reluctance towards the 'marketisation' of telecommunication services enhanced the robustness of incumbent structures.

Even though one cannot literally speak of a regime *crisis* demanding change, *technological progress* and greater intensity of *globalisation* provoked a new perspective on traditional, monopolistic telecommunications in the public as well as the political perception. According to this new view, staying with the incumbent structures meant both letting enormous potential for economic growth and employment slip past as well as endangering the competitiveness of German industries. Despite continuing unease about DBP's inability to comply with customers' demands, the dysfunction of the regime was not suspected until new communication technologies came up. Certainly, this helped to break up the former anti-reform coalition by promising new business for the incumbent 'purveyors to the court'. However, I should emphasise that the perceived 'crisis' at that time was ultimately provoked *externally* and it is unlikely that without technological developments revolutionising offices all over the world, the German telecommunication monopoly of DBP would have been seriously challenged. After all, in 1984 the federal government still believed DBP was able to develop exclusively and implement the modern ISDN technology. Why then, one might speculate, would any government consider ordinary telephony deserved liberalisation? Rather, Germany, as well as many other European countries would probably have tried to prolong the incumbent national monopoly regimes a little longer, had not another actor come on the scene: the EC Commission.

The concern with telecommunications and its ability to cope with technological developments in an increasingly globalised international economy was intensified and ultimately accelerated by the politics of *European integration* for two reasons. First, the EC Commission viewed technological progress in telecommunications as a chance to bring telecommunications increasingly under its jurisdiction. Consequently, it initiated several important reform steps. Second, the EC Council was used by the German executive, especially in the first half of the 1990s, to circumvent deadlocked institutions at home. I would argue that the relative impact of 'Europe' (both as an arena and an actor in the telecommunications policy) had increased and become particularly decisive for the final stage of *Postreform III*. At this time, the German federal government had not only fully realised that, for example, German unification needed an influx of private capital to finance telecommunication infrastructures in the East, but also understood that an enormous potential for German industry lay dormant. 'Unionisation' (*Vergemeinschaftung*) of telecommunication regulation has, however, not been extended to the whole sector and still remains limited to framework legislation as well as technical harmonisation. Nevertheless, as considerable parts of European law are directly applicable in the member states, 'Europe' must not only be seen as a major force accounting for the shape of the regulatory regime now incumbent in Germany, but also as a primary source of regulation itself. In a sense, Europe has been a functional equivalent to what the BVerfG performed in broadcasting regulation, that is serving as both a source and a resource of telecommunication regulation in Germany.

We even have to add a third dimension of Europe accounting for regulatory change in Germany: *policy-learning* from European neighbours, especially learning from the United Kingdom's experience, as well as that of other more advanced 'regulatory states'. Both the agency and particularly the compliance aspects of the newly set up regulatory regime of the 1996 legislation included several particularities – from 'price caps' to the 'essential facilities' doctrine – which can be traced back to Anglo-American origins in particular. Nevertheless, no 'model copying' took place. Rather, successful institutions and instruments from regulatory regimes abroad had to be harmonised with, first, the traditions of the German administrative and legal culture and second, the specific pre-market situation in Germany. By the latter, I mean that concrete details of the regime as established in 1996 were always *problem-driven*, which of course, is not necessarily a surprising discovery.

Re-assessment on behalf of the regulated in the strict sense of the word could not take place, as there were no *regulated* market players. However, the thought behind this *topoi* might still be of some relevance in two respects. First, as mentioned earlier, if one views German suppliers to DBP as indirectly 'regulated' by the traditional regulatory regime, their changed attitude towards reform, starting in the late 1970s, might well be considered a case in point here. Second, after the first step of telecommunication reform was taken, a certain intra-sectoral dynamism developed, which extended to DBP Telekom. The former monopolist's executive level was quickly replaced by more market-oriented business experts from outside the organisation. While this replacement policy was ultimately pursued as a political project to make the public monopoly fit for the world market, it induced a certain level of intra-organisational power to press for greater independence by way of privatisation.

Finally, if we look at both the regulatory institutions at work *and* the procedural formulas they apply, it becomes obvious that the *legacy* of German administrative culture in the public service perpetuates a certain 'traditionalism' even where new instruments and organisational units have been set up. The system of 'decision-taking chambers' has legally been linked to the 'law of administrative procedures' (*Verwaltungsverfahrensgesetz (VwVfG)*) and so have virtually all of their actions vis à vis market entry, price regulation, network access and so on. RegTP has been inspired by the Anglo-American practice of sectoral regulation through independent commissions, but the 1996 'revolution' has not broken with the public legal and administrative tradition. Still, regulators are substantially bound by the law and their decisions are subject to judicial review. In the German legal culture, the latter two points seem to represent an insoluble unity, which explicates what the *Rechtsstaatsprinzip* (only insufficiently translated by 'rule of law') means in essence.

Notes

1 The history of 1993 is in fact an interesting object of study, because the Council opted for 'option 3', i.e. full liberalisation of telephony by 1998, even though the Commission favoured 'option 4', intending only cross-border liberalisation of telephony. See Zydorek (1998: 159). We can only speculate about the Commission's motives to prefer a more modest course of reform at this time. However, the incident exemplifies that it would be too simplistic to identify the EU Commission as the 'engine' pushing the EU Council and all member states towards a Europe-wide, liberalised telecommunications regime. Rather, European institutions and national governments have interacted and promoted the liberalisation process at different stages.

2 Zukunftsprogramm Informationstechnik (1984), printed in BT– Drs. 10/1281 of 11.4.1984.

3 DBP Telekom's newly won freedom was partly limited, in particular, by the participation of other departments (*Ressortbeteiligung*), as a substitute for the abandoned *Postverwaltungsrat*, which served to articulate the *Länder* (and other) interests. Limitation of freedom was also generated by a *Infrastrukturrat* and a powerful, common board of executives from the three branches of DBP (telecommunications, postal services, and banking).

4 However, as reported by a former officer at the ministry, this hypothesis is fully wrong. The procedural safeguards against such an industrial policy approach, explained elsewhere in this study, had already been applied at that time. The hypothesis as presented in the literature lacks empirical references and is solely grounded on speculation vis à vis 'rational' behaviour in bureaucracies.

5 *Handelsblatt* of 20 February 1989

6 It has also been argued by an RegTP officer that the federal government put a certain emphasis on a European compromise due to the German presidency in the EU Council at that time. The presidency was considered to be employed to spread liberalisation of telecommunications all over Europe. Accordingly, as far as the content of the liberalisation project in the EU is concerned, the German ministry was always one step ahead. In that sense, Europe has here not been a source, but a resource in a double sense: promoting reform in both Europe and Germany. It should, however, be mentioned that in the legislative process afterwards, parliamentary opposition in the *Bundestag* did not play a crucial role. The time of hard confrontation was over.

7 See also the *Bundestag* postal services and telecommunications committee report of 27 June1994, BT– Drs. 12/8060, p. 175.

8 See, for instance, WIK (1998): Ein analytisches Kostenmodell für das Ortsnetz, in: ABl. RegTP 1998, 1163. This report, contributing to solving the cost model problem for the local loop and hence 'price regulation', exemplifies that considerable work on fundamentals, involving scientific research, has been delegated to an semi-independent institution. Nevertheless, the very fact of publishing the report in RegTP's official publication (*Amtsblatt*), where decisions and other official orders are published, illustrates the report's significance for RegTP.

9 In §§ 2,3,4 NZV, the decree stipulates that market-dominant network operators have to grant access to their networks and comply thereby with the following principles: unbundling of service (i.e. no obligation to buy packages); collocation (i.e. providing for physical or virtual access to related facilities etc. where necessary to technically realize network access); and information duties (i.e. providing the accessing competitor with the information necessary to effectively use its access rights).

5

Broadcasting

a) Origins, sources and core questions of broadcasting regulation

Broadcasting has always been subject to one dilemma, namely whether it is to be assigned to the public or to the private sphere. On the one hand, broadcasting can be seen as a form of economic service, whose price is best measured by relative costs of commercial time on air. This represents the American approach, which understands broadcasting primarily as a business. On the other hand, broadcasting is a mass medium, whose reach and effectiveness beats newspapers and other printed forms in modern society. Recognising the dangers resulting from such power to influence people, it has been argued that broadcasting cannot be left to private forces alone. Rather, its use must be directed towards the 'common good' and controlled by the state to prevent misuse. This approach to the regulation of broadcasting is often to be found in Europe. However, there is a third line of argument: if there is only a limited number of programmes available, because frequencies are restricted by technical barriers, and, furthermore, if one accepts that there is a public interest in granting the state a say in broadcasting due to the above rationale, then one must question whether one can be sure that the state is not abusing broadcasting as an instrument for political propaganda.

Debate on the order and regulation of broadcasting in Germany has seen all of these arguments appearing time and again. While technical developments have eased to some extent the difficulties resulting from the public–private dichotomy, the general consensus regarding the role of the state in regulating broadcasting has not been challenged. However, as will be seen later, except for the period of NS rule between 1933 and 1945 (Diller 1980), there has always been a semi-statal, semi-societal mixture in broadcasting, which makes it extremely difficult to keep both spheres clearly separated. Even after the admission of private broadcasting in 1984 and the creation of the so-called 'dual order' (*Duale Ordnung*), the private and the public sphere have continued to intermingle.

While the state has assumed supervisory powers over private broadcasters since their licensing, societal forces have always had their place in what is called 'public broadcasting'. In fact, the latter was and is more of a system of societal self-governance within a statal, public law framework.

The regulatory legacy of Weimar – decentralisation, statal control and private entrepreneurship

Broadcasting in Germany started as a highly decentralised project, introducing a new technology on the initiative and under the control of the German Postal Services (*Deutsche Reichspost* (DRP)). While DRP intended to provide for the transmission network only, nine regional broadcasting corporations were founded to organise programmes to be broadcast.

These regional corporations were mostly funded by private capital (Albert 1997: 348), even though regional public bodies partly contributed (Führer 1997: 23–25). It seems safe to assume that these privately owned broadcasting companies came into existence only because the state (here, the ministry for postal services, *Reichspostministerium*) did not want to invest capital itself. However, despite their legal position as private companies, the nine regional companies had no chance to develop as free enterprises. In fact, by withholding broadcasting licences DRP 'blackmailed' the broadcasting corporations into transferring preference shares to DRP and the Empire, which ensured they achieved free dominating control of all corporations (Lerg 1970). However, the distribution of shares, which provided DRP with power over private broadcasting, was less clear-cut, illustrating both internal conflicts within the executive (between *Reichspostministerium* (with DRP) and Ministry of the Interior (*Reichsinnenministerium*) (RIM)) and the external conflict between the *Reich* and the *Länder* governments.

All shares were held as registered shares (*Namensaktien*). By insisting on that restriction, DRP ensured that it had a final veto on share transfers. It prohibited sales to foreigners, and tended to buy them itself. All of this makes it clear that the private corporations, even though founded by private sponsors in private legal form, soon became dependent vassals of DRP. Private capital owners viewed their investment purely as a money-making instrument and DRP provided for a range of incentives to keep private investors quiet (Bauer 1993). The system has been described by Führer (1997: 18) as one of a 'mixed economy' (*gemischt-wirtschaftliches System*), but more precisely it represents an arrangement of *private capital – full state control* regulation.

The central institution in the regulatory arrangement set up under the control of DRP was the *Reichs-Rundfunk-Gesellschaft* (RRG). Formally founded by the broadcasting corporations in 1925 to deal with common matters and problems of all broadcasting companies (RRG 1926: 7), it was designed to serve as a self-regulatory agency. However, DRP gained control over RRG in 1926 after threatening to withhold licences for the broadcasting corporations. It systematically transformed RRG into a semi-autonomous regulator, exercising almost full regulatory control. While DRP retained only legal affairs, scaling of fees and matters of technical transmission, it entrusted RRG with all other competencies. RRG used this potential quite successfully and developed from a small bureau of 30 employees in 1926/7 to a fully-fledged office of 361 staff in 1931 (RRG 1926 to 1932).

RRG had two directors, but the central figure was the so-called 'Broadcasting Commissioner' (*Rundfunk-Kommissar*) Bredow. Formally supposed to supervise RRG, he effectively controlled broadcasting regulation. Bredow was a former top ministerial officer, but as commissioner he was not bound by civil service law. Historical research indicates that Bredow had an extremely powerful position, not only with regard to RRG, its directors and staff, and the regulated broadcasting companies, but also towards DRP and the ministry (Führer 1997: 33–34 and 119–122). Nevertheless, the commissioner has to be understood also as a communicator from one actor to the other, an arbitrator articulating respective interests and searching for settlement.

The courts played only a minor role in broadcasting regulation. Between 1926 and 1931 a couple of decisions touched on the question of whether broadcasting should represent entertainment only or a 'commodity', such as public transportation (Vollmann 1936: 29–30). The problem was relevant for tenants' rights to install radio masts on their roofs, including all aspects of liability in case of damages. The question was considered of great importance for the spread of radios in Germany, which had been a 'developing country' in terms of broadcasting until 1930. The *Landgericht Königsberg* was the first higher court in 1929 to stand up in opposition to the supreme court (*Reichsgericht*) and consider broadcasting a commodity. It paved the way for similar decisions in the years to come.

Even in this semi-statal, semi-private mixed system of broadcasting and broadcasting regulation there had already been an arrangement for financial equalisation (*Finanzausgleich*). The broadcasting corporations contributed membership fees to RRG to finance RRG's work. However, the smaller, weaker companies in Stuttgart, Breslau and Königsberg were reimbursed (Führer 1997: 148–152). Nevertheless, despite financial problems in the weak corporations and in spite of the fact that de-centralisation was no longer necessary for technical reasons in the late 1920s, the regionalised structure of German broadcasting remained until 1932. Former attempts by RRG to merge corporations, build broadcasting alliances (*Sendegemeinschaften*) or at least foster the exchange of programmes were by and large unsuccessful. Whilst RRG became more and ever more powerful until 1932, when it was formally nationalised and incorporated into the general administration of the *Reich*, it was unable to prevail over German regionalism.

In short, the beginning of broadcasting regulation in Germany is characterised by central state initiation and continuous influence on the one side, but also private capital engagement and regional inertia on the other. The tension of interests could only be held in balance, because private shareholders viewed their stake in broadcasting mainly as an investment. DRP respected the latter group's interest in shareholder value in order to secure its control over a new sector, which it considered crucial not only for fiscal reasons. While formally entrusted with feudal power, DRP delegated most of its authority to RRG and accepted the commissioner's policy. However, RRG was not just an extension of DRP, but retained the profile of a semi-independent regulatory agency, based on the personal authority of Hans Bredow, which provided for the exchange and (financial) equalisation among the member broadcasting companies.

Federalism, imported regulation and the significance of the judiciary

After the Second World War, it was questionable whether the *Länder* or the federal level was constitutionally empowered to regulate broadcasting. While the allies left Germany with a decentralised, yet *Länder*-boundaries-cutting public broadcasting system, it needed a decision by the Federal Constitutional Court to clarify the assignment of constitutional powers between the federal and the *Länder* levels. However, as will be seen later, the court did not only effectively ban the federal government from interference, but also took much of the power away from the *Länder*. The court became the single most important ally of public broadcasters and a major source of regulation. It defined the framework for broadcasting in Germany, within which the *Länder* had only partial discretion to live out 'diversity'. The court restricted their room for manoeuvre not only by introducing substantial regulatory norms, but also by requiring inter-*Länder* consent on some of the remaining issues of responsibility, which had not been assigned to the public broadcasting corporations themselves. Therefore, in a sense, the victory of the *Länder* in 1961 was only a defeat for the federal government.

Interestingly enough, as we shall see, the European level has not been as influential as it was in other sectors. Again, this is partly due to judicial activism, if not 'protectionism' when dealing with a broadcasting order whose fundamentals stem from a time when the memories of political propaganda by the NS government and the dangers of 'laissez-faire' policies for mass media were still vivid. When this attitude will disappear is impossible to predict. Perhaps the rise of digital technology and the merger of broadcasting with modern information technologies, such as the Internet, will effectively undermine the legacy of an order shaped and protected by the judiciary.

b) Legitimacy: freedom or cultural responsibility?

Regulatory principles in broadcasting have hardly changed over the past five decades. This is the quintessential message after analysing the history of broadcasting in Germany. Most of these principles have been defined in a series of BVerfG decisions and their core elements were already included in the very first court ruling of 1961. If anything, new regulatory goals have been added to old ones, without superseding the latter in any way. Whenever politics tried to alter the list of legitimate regulatory goals, as defined by the judiciary, the BVerfG appeared on the scene and stopped the presumed demolition of its carefully crafted framework. In this section, I will list and describe the regulatory principles, both the traditional and the recent ones, illuminating the extraordinary degree of continuity. I argue that the incumbent 'dual broadcasting system' is an unavoidable consequence of BVerfG ruling on the one hand and technological development on the other[1]. One could well put forward the claim that politics have played no primary role as far as the fundamental regulatory outline goes. In fact, politics was not given appreciable discretion by the court in that matter. As to the research design of this study, I argue that cases in point have only been found for *equality* and *security*. *Efficiency* has not played a significant role, although broadcasting is increasingly seen as a business with macroeconomic consequences, especially since the EC Commission's Greenbook of 1984 (Schuler-Harms 1995: 18).

In order to describe and analyse the principles governing broadcasting regulation, as almost exclusively set up by the BVerfG, we need to distinguish as follows. First, what are the rationales for 'broadcasting exceptionalism'? These findings help us to understand the framework of principles for broadcasting, which have, in fact, never changed. Second, what are the principles governing public broadcasting regulation on the one hand and private broadcasting regulation on the other? By comparing similarities and dissimilarities the more fundamental consideration of what legitimises both broadcasting sectors will become clear.

Public service philosophy

Broadcasting, no matter whether public or private, is in both public perception, political decision-making and court rulings bound into a public service philosophy. Despite the rising importance of the economic aspects of commercial TV and radio, no one seems willing to abandon a certain public caring attitude for the sake of a presumably more efficient market logic. If anything, the observable lowering of quality standards (particularly in private TV) has even caused proponents of a private broadcasting system to become more critical regarding their former deregulation approach. Since the 1961 decision of the BVerfG (BVerfGE 12, 205), which considered broadcasting to be a commodity beyond market allocation, a public service which demands more than just giving people what they want to see, ranks among the unassailable truths of German broadcasting regulation. Even the European Court of Justice, traditionally a driving force towards European harmonisation and the opening-up of national markets to European competition in many sectors, has acknowledged that broadcasting is exceptional, hence partly exempt from the general free access philosophy (Hoffmann 1995: 634–637). Of course, the BVerfG (until BVerfGE 57, 295) had referred to the shortage of frequencies as a technical reason to restrict the number of broadcasters, thus excluding private suppliers. But it was clear from the beginning that 'broadcasting exceptionalism' (i.e. the necessity to apply other standards than those of usual markets for goods and services), and public broadcasting in particular, is not a choice to be left to political discretion. Consequently, while deregulation of telecommunication and other markets in the 1980s and 1990s has been linked to a new understanding of these services, which allowed for concentration almost exclusively on technical questions and problems of efficient competition, broadcasting has not seen such re-evaluation.

However, the above does not necessarily imply that broadcasting is *not* an economic activity. It simply states that it is a possible economic activity which need not obey market laws. Broadcasting is a matter of demand and supply, yet both aspects somehow need to be defined and realised differently than prescribed by the usual 'buy and sell' logic. To understand 'broadcasting exceptionalism' in both public, political and juridical debate one might refer to Eberle (1997: 358), who argued that broadcasting is both a 'cultural asset' (*Kulturgut*) and an 'economic asset' (*Wirtschaftsgut*). This not only means that broadcasting has become an integral element of culture in Western societies, but also that it serves as a communicator in society, providing for an opportunity to present and participate in ideas, opinions and all forms of cultural or political activities. Thus, it is important for society as a whole to ensure general access to broadcasting, as it fulfils an essential, socio-political function. Public broadcasters like to emphasise the 'meritorious character' of 'high quality' broadcasting (*meritorisches Gut*), whose relative importance for society exceeds what the market would actually pay for (Oeller 1989: 112).

This attitude, as described above, is more or less the rationale of broadcasting regulation given by the BVerfG in a series of decisions between 1961 and

1995. It had important implications for the structure of the broadcasting market, before and after private broadcasters had been granted entry. Legislators have carefully watched the courts' outline of arguments and kept central parts of their broadcasting acts close to BVerfG language. Fortunately, from a research perspective, the functioning of the BVerfG as the chief regulator of broadcasting well into the 1980s (and some might argue into the 1990s) has provided us with a well-documented blueprint of regulatory principles, goals and rationales. However, no reform has ever been due to court ruling. Rather, the BVerfG had been used in these occasions as a resource to stop challenges to the *status quo*. The court has often lived up to these expectations. On other occasions, especially in the 1980s and 1990s, the judiciary has increasingly adopted a strategy of self-restraint – without abandoning any principle set in past decisions. In a sense, the court has since diminished its role to some degree as a source of regulatory principles.

The new regulatory approach since 1984, the *dual system approach*, is an almost inevitable consequence of BVerfG ruling. I would argue that whatever national politics had intended in the 1980s and 1990s, the court's outline of what standards any broadcasting system has to live up to in constitutional terms would have rendered any other solution void. The most important argument in support of this hypothesis is the following: the court has almost exclusively defined and cemented the fundamentals on which politics has been building its models. The principles set up revolve around the concepts of 'diversity/pluralism of opinions' (*Meinungsvielfalt*), 'basic supply' (*Grundversorgung*) and the 'freedom to broadcast' (*Rundfunkfreiheit*). From the latter it follows that potential private broadcasters cannot really be prevented from starting their businesses, unless, first, pluralism of opinions is endangered (which is not the case, as long as public broadcasting operates the way it has since the Second World War) or second, technical restrictions do not allow for more than the incumbent, public broadcasting services. This had been, more or less, a valid argument until the late 1970s or early 1980s. Since then, technological progress has rendered it obsolete. As a result of this kind of thinking, it follows that in the 1980s there was no longer any reason to exclude private players from broadcasting. Of course, certain political forces had already been trying to gain admission. But even if they had not done so, private broadcasters would have had a case to bring before the BVerfG. According to its consistent logic regarding the rest, the court would have had no other choice but to order the *Länder* to construct a framework which would enable both public broadcasting to survive and develop according the court's regulatory intentions, and also private broadcasters to make use of their constitutional rights. What else is the *dual broadcasting system* as we see it today?

Broadcasting, democracy, and pluralism

The above implies that a comprehensive doctrine developed by the BVerfG over several decades forms the core of both public and private broadcasting regulation. The starting point was the court's *medium and factor-theory* (BVerfGE 12, 205 (260) and 57, 295 (320)). That is, broadcasting does not only serve as a communicator of information, but it also keeps public debate alive, substantially shaping public opinion (e.g., Preuss Neudorf 1993: 49–50). The latter point refers to the fact that broadcasting reaches enormous numbers of people; the news presented on TV or radio sets agendas and is likely to influence the way people think about certain issues. This is, of course, an omnipresent problem of modern mass communication and its dangers had become obvious in the Third Reich. It is hardly surprising then that the court found broadcasting to be of essential importance to sustain democracy.

The 'freedom to broadcast' (*Rundfunkfreiheit*), which is included implicitly in Art. 5 of the Basic Law, stands in juxtaposition to this 'functional' approach presented above. How can an individual's right of defence against the state (*Abwehrrecht*) be reconciled with a 'socialised' concept of the very act of broadcasting, loaded with a large amount of *raison d'état* (*démocratique*)? The BVerfG (BVerfGE 57, 295 (320)) opted for re-definition of the fundamental right, making it a 'serving freedom' (*dienende Freiheit*). The freedom to broadcast is bound by its function in society (i.e. contributing to a stable democracy). It ultimately serves a higher purpose than just individual self-realisation. In later decisions, after the dual system had become a reality in German broadcasting, the BVerfG gave its attention to the so-called 'subjective' meaning of this fundamental right (Niepalla 1990: 10, 14–16); with this more liberal-individualistic view it has since acknowledged that broadcasting need not be restricted to a *purely* public service for the common good any further. Nevertheless, pluralism, and the balance thereof, is still to be pursued, even though single broadcasters are not to be held directly accountable. A macro-perspective has thus replaced the former micro-perspective with regard to regulatory goals.

Pluralism, i.e. the diversity of opinions presented in the radio and on TV, is an imminent consequence of the medium and factor-theory. All 'socially significant groups' need to have a say in both decision-making and the programmes themselves (BVerfGE 12, 205). Society is thus not only viewed as an audience of broadcasting, but also as a source of the programming. Pluralism does, however, also imply that no single group may become dominant (BVerfGE 73, 118). 'Balance' (*Ausgewogenheit*) is needed in order to prevent broadcasting from falling into the hands of a few. This is a regulatory goal which can be subsumed under *equality*. As will be explained later, it can be *implemented* in different ways.

Finally, the court developed the idea of 'basic supply' (*Grundversorgung*)[2]. Originally proposed by Herrmann (1975: 332–334), the concept of *Grundversorgung* became not only the ultimate source of legitimacy for public broadcasting corporations, but also one of their most efficient weapons in public debate. It is closely related to the 'classical programme assignment' doctrine (*klassischer Programmauftrag*), stating that, to ensure the integrity of the democratic process of shaping opinions (Libertus 1991), it is necessary to provide information, cultural, educational and entertaining programmes for *everyone* (BVerwGE 75, 67 (74)). Herrmann justified the concept of *Grundversorgung* as a constitutional 'must' by referring to both the 'democratic principle' (*Demokratieprinzip*) and the 'principle of the social welfare state' (*Sozialstaatsprinzip*). The BVerfG has adopted this view, picking up Smend's (1928) 'integration theory' (*Integrationslehre*), according to which the state is subject to constant political change. It follows that the dynamic process of opinion-forming, a prerequisite for acceptance and participation of 'enlightened' citizens in a democracy, is crucial. *Everyone* must have equal access to the process of opinion-forming (Gersdorf 1991: 62–63), which implies the principle of 'justice in communicative supply' (*kommunikative Versorgungsgerechtigkeit*). This includes a state duty to both provide for adequate technical systems and transmitters to reach everyone and offer broadcasting at a socially affordable cost. Low-income classes thus have the right to receive TV and radio at a lower licence fee rate. Obviously, the *Grundversorgung* doctrine is essentially an *equality* goal of regulating broadcasting. It has never been given up by the BVerfG and has been publicly and politically accepted as one of the fundamentals of broadcasting regulation in Germany.

Connecting public and private broadcasting – common principles

Quite early on, the BVerfG has also developed a doctrine whose indispensible principles private broadcasting has to meet. While the courts have lowered standards in later decisions, some have survived. Among them are two important groups:

- adherence to the journalistic code of honour (*publizistische Leitgrundsätze*), such as objectivity, truthfulness and fairness;
- consumer protection (*Verbraucherschutz*), protection of children and young persons (*Jugendschutz*), protection of personality (*Persönlichkeitsschutz*) and protection of personal data (*Datenschutz*).

While the first seems to be related somewhat to the more general intention of providing a balanced range of programmes (which, of course, requires a certain degree of honesty and fairness on behalf of all suppliers), the second brings in a new aspect. It aims at implementing certain socially desirable goals *through* broadcasting, although they are essentially independent from it. They fall under the category of ***security***. While 'pluralism' is a principle applied on the macro-level, these 'protection clauses' listed above are to be respected by every broadcaster, no matter whether public or private. In a way, they might be considered the *micro-perspective* counterpart to 'diversity' and 'pluralism'.

What so far remains unfulfilled is *efficiency*. In fact, I argue that it does not play a significant role, even though economic aspects of broadcasting have certainly gained importance since the 1980s. First of all, just because an economic perspective now exists, this does not necessarily imply that 'efficiency' has got a stake, too. Allowing for economic freedom to extend to broadcasting is not the same as fostering competition among suppliers in order to get lower prices or better quality. If anything, court rulings and political action (since the 1991 and especially 1997 *Rundfunkstaatsvertrag*) have been aware of the concentration problem (with just two media groups dominating German TV) from a pluralism point of view. They are, however, not so much concerned with economic efficiency.

EU policy is different. In the above-mentioned Green Book (1984) of the Commission, broadcasting is considered a market to be brought together into one single European market. For the Commission, economic measures, such as the increase in employment and free access to markets within the community, are at the core. Some *Länder* governments have adopted part of that view and consider their respective broadcasting regulation policy more or less as serving industrial policy goals (Benz 1997: 448). This is, of course, less a matter of 'regulatory principles' – they are pretty much the same all over Germany, due to the *Rundfunkstaatsvertrag* – than of implementation and practice by the *Landesmedienanstalten*. By deciding in 1986 that 'essential' matters of broadcasting regulation have to be dealt with in a joint effort by the *Länder*, the BVerfG had effectively ruled out any fundamentally different approaches to regulating the dual broadcasting system. The omnipresent 'obsession' with federalist diversity and regional distinctiveness was hence ignored for the sake of rescuing the court's sovereignty in deciding upon fundamental regulatory principles. What becomes clear is, however, that broadcasting regulation is being shaped either by the judiciary, by *Länder governments* (executives) in co-ordinated efforts, or by the regulatory agencies' *practice*.

As far as the impact of EU broadcasting policy is concerned, the 'freedom to broadcast' and a certain degree of mutual acceptance of regulatory standards have either been introduced to or strengthened within the German broadcasting system (Mestmäcker *et al.* 1990). Ultimately, the goal is to create a level playing field for European broadcasters by gradually eliminating national obstacles. Even though a higher degree of efficiency in broadcasting, however measured, might be a consequence of a – European-wide – equal opportunity approach, the intention is to have *equality* of suppliers.

In short, private broadcasting regulation is influenced by the principles mentioned above in three ways. First, the *Grundversorgung* doctrine, which actually concerns public broadcasting, has an indirect impact on private broadcasting, because it defines the scope of privileges granted to the public competitors. Second, the *Meinungsvielfalt* doctrine, aiming at ensuring pluralism of the views and opinions presented in broadcasting, and governing admission and supervision of private broadcasters, as will be seen in the following sections of this chapter. Although originally designed to justify the monopoly of public service corporations, it now serves as a general principle for regulators to be applied in a macro-perspective. Third, the 'protection clauses' have also been set up as standards in both public and private broadcasting, but they apply to each broadcasting station separately. Interestingly enough, as opposed to most other 'deregulated' sectors, even the private players newly operating in the broadcasting market are not significantly regulated by referring to *efficiency* goals, however they may be defined. Generally speaking, economic factors are only of secondary importance and where *Länder* governments have aimed at using their regulatory authority to engage in industrial policy-making, the BVerfG has put up obstacles, which have effectively prevented strong regional diversity of regulatory regimes.

As the rationales and goals presented above come from judicial reasoning, the boundary between the categories of 'legitimacy' as a *rationale* and 'legitimacy' as a *political goal* is less clear-cut. While all of them, or course, refer to legal constitutional principles as rationale, they certainly represent a quite distinct constitutionally based policy for regulating mass media. Generally speaking, three features are striking. First, the court was serious about federalism and *Länder* powers in the 1960s. Second, the court realised the need to balance different legal values (*Rechtsgüter*) right from the beginning, therefore introducing an option for private broadcasting as well. Third, it was decided that, once established, private broadcasting and more importantly, the regulation thereof, should work more or less similarly to public broadcasting regulation as regards state independence. Finally, the BVerfG's decisions have also produced winners and losers. Public broadcasting is clearly on the winning side, and so are the self-administered LMAs, regulating private broadcasting. Both claims will be illustrated in the following section. (See Table 5.1.)

Table 5.1: *Legitimacy* in public and private broadcasting

	Public broadcasting	Private broadcasting
Rationale	- Diversity of opinion - Basic supply Protection clause (meritorious good)	- Diversity of opinion Protection clauses (meritorious good)
Political goal	Equality and security	Equality and security
Winner	All public broadcasting corporations	LMAs

c) Agency: the Dual Broadcasting System a double-standard regime?

The regulators as agents are to be found on several levels, with quite different degrees of autonomy and a variety of organisational forms with regard to (internal) decision-making. First of all, the *dual broadcasting system* has brought about two spheres of regulation, including different regulatory agents and modes. Both spheres overlap, however, in certain areas. While the 'super-regulator' of public broadcasting, the judiciary, has extended this function to the private system and remained therein since 1984, the regulatory institutions inferior to the BVerfG follow different logics. They can be categorised alongside the conceptual opposites of 'internal pluralism' (*Binnenpluralismus*) and 'external pluralism' (*Außenpluralismus*): regulatory control in public broadcasting corporations is substantially provided internally (i.e. *Rundfunk-* or *Fernsehräte*), whereas private broadcasters face an external regulator (i.e. the *Landesmedienanstalten*). In both cases, the *Länder* have formal authority to legislate and in fact, 'broadcasting councils' (as part of the respective public broadcasting corporation) and 'state media agencies' are creations of the *Länder*. Viewed from this perspective, *Länder* executives and legislators could be seen as 'mezzanine regulators'. Regarding public broadcasting, the *Länder* have reserved certain rights over the organisation of broadcasting corporations or the additional assignment of new frequencies. However, to make things more complicated, I argue that, according to BVerfG ruling, the *Länder* (and their *Landesmedienanstalten*) are not really free to fully experience regional diversity. Rather, we observe *limping federalism* with regard to several issues in broadcasting regulation and its regulators; not only because the 'freedom to experiment' (and to be different) is only 'on loan' for a limited period until the court presents its position, but also because of the BVerfG 1986 opinion, according to which essential questions have to be dealt with co-operatively. The *Länder*, creators of the *Landesmedienanstalten* (LMAs), are 'condemned' to 'cooperative federalism' (*kooperativer Föderalismus*) in many fields – and the LMAs have learned to live with it. Similarly, the financing of public broadcasting must be decided cooperatively. However, there are still less publicly-debated domaines where the *Länder* have adopted distinctive regulatory arrangements.

Public broadcasting

Public broadcasting in Germany is not to be confused with state activity in a classical sense. Rather, the public system has a semi-statal, semi-private status, dangling somewhere between society and state. However, with regard to decision-making in programming, society is much closer than the state. The latter serves merely as an umbrella, under which 'socially significant groups' determine programmes, staffing and other fundamental matters in the running of a broadcasting corporation. Even though this is the ideal presented by the BVerfG, reality has proved to be more politicised than the court was able to acknowledge in the first place. Someone has to define what is 'socially significant' and after all, the state has to provide *funding*, giving it a certain, if jurisprudentially limited, degree of discretion. Moreover, similar to the setting of fees, *frequencies* are not within the broadcasters' authority and are also assigned by the state. Finally, matters of internal organisation, such as the choice between a 'Director's Constitution' (*Intendantenverfassung*) and a 'Board of Directors' Constitution' (*Direktoralverfassung*), are left to state legislators.

After a brief description of the key elements in public broadcasting in Germany, I will analyse these features by first emphasising the regulatory significance of the 'broadcasting councils' as *internal regulators*, showing aspects of both party-political orientation and societal integration, second, the regulatory importance of the *Länder* regarding organisation and finance in particular, and third, the ultimate power of the judiciary as a 'super-regulatory authority'.

The Institutional setting for regulation at a glance

The new broadcasting system after the Second World War was a mixture of the German tradition of regionalism and decentralisation on the one hand and the mainly British conception of a public service (Hoffmann-Riem 1991) and yet a broadcasting network freed from the state on the other. Even during the final days of the Second World War, the British military were broadcasting in occupied areas in May 1945 (Halefeldt 1989: 20). Several others followed suit over the next few months. Yet already in 1946/7, the allies had started to slowly withdraw from broadcasting control, preparing both German broadcasting management and politicians for their own independent form of broadcasting (Schmücker 1969). Before the Federal Republic of Germany was founded in May 1949, six public broadcasting corporations (*öffentlich-rechtliche Rundfunkanstalten*), each legally independent, both from each other and from the state, were established and served the public in their regional monopolies.

These six corporations formed the core group of the later 'work group of public broadcasting corporations of the Federal Republic of Germany' (*Arbeitsgemeinschaft der öffentlich-rechtlichen Rundfunkanstalten der Bundesrepublik Deutschland*), the so-called ARD, founded in 1950[3]. ARD was started as a formally loose group of broadcasters still independent but with a common statute[4]. And it kept the status of a group under private law when the *Sender Freies* Berlin (SFB) in 1953 and the *Saarländischer Rundfunk* (SR) in 1957 joined the group. One of the most important broadcasting goals of the ARD was to establish a national television programme in 1953 (Bausch 1983), which all member corporations would be contributing to.

ARD shows a number of features that have lasted right up to today. First and foremost, the member broadcasting corporations have always been independent from each other. ARD is not the head of a group which dominates its members. Rather, the founding member corporations have carefully crafted a regime that provides for central decision-making only, where co-operation is indispensible. The six monthly rotation of the presidency and the stipulation of unanimous consent laid down in the original 1950 statutes (Diller 1975: 39), have ensured that no corporation can take over. After NDWR was divided into NDR and WDR in 1954/5, the problem of corporate dominance within ARD had certainly diminished anyway. Nevertheless, it should be mentioned that the disintegration of NDWR was rather exceptional, as in the course of broadcasting history, especially after German unification (Rossen 1992), mergers between small and medium-sized public broadcasters have become more common.

Looking at internal organisation (Eberle 1997: 360–361), public broadcasters followed the model of internal pluralism (*Binnenpluralismus*). This means that each corporation has a broadcasting council (*Rundfunkrat*), which reflects societal groups and meanings, to decide on questions of fundamental importance, such as programme structure or staff. Mostly representatives from 'socially significant groups' make up this institution. Even though the arrangement fits perfectly into German traditions of corporatism, it was an idea brought in from the United States, which preferred incorporating societal representation over political appointments (Halefeldt 1989: 22–23). However, vesting 'executive' power in a strong director (*Intendant*) was introduced by the British. The director is responsible for the programme as a whole to both the public and the broadcasting council (Neuffer 1975). As opposed to members of the council, the director has a full-time job with better access to information. Thus, as far as detailed questions of daily business are concerned, the director holds an extremely powerful position.

ARD is, for a number of reasons, a unique institution, quite foreign to both the German legal and political cultures. For one thing, the new conception of *independent* broadcasting, created and supported, yet not dominated by the state, had been something quite novel in Germany. And it was not politically accepted in the first place. Especially politicians had to get used to the idea of state-sponsored, yet state-free broadcasting, funded by public money (Bausch 1975: 19). Even a new legal form for organising public broadcasting had to be found. Here, the British were certainly more dominant than the Americans, even though the latter had less of a problem with German regionalism and decentralisation. Secondly, the foundation of ARD shows that these six independent broadcasting services realised the need for co-operation to solve technical problems and the like. It uncovers a widespread fear among broadcasting managements of regulatory intervention by the federal government. In this first period, which lasted until 1961, it was not clear to what extent the federal government would try to regain authority. The Basic Law (*Grundgesetz* (GG)) of the Federal Republic of Germany vested postal services and telecommunications in the federal government, thus providing it with an argument to assume regulatory competencies in broadcasting, at least as far as organisational matters (*Organisationshoheit*) are concerned (Steininger 1975). On the other hand, the *Länder* argued that, first, all competencies not specifically granted to the federal government belonged to them (Art. 30 GG) and, second, if anything, broadcasting was a matter of culture, which had always, and without any doubt, been under *Länder* authority (*Kulturhoheit*). Nevertheless, both *Länder* governments and broadcasting corporations were pretty sure that the federal government would eventually assume certain rights, at least by passing a framework law, re-ordering the rather accidental emergence of broadcasting corporations in Germany.

In fact, the federal government started several attempts to introduce legislation (e.g., BT-Drs. 1/4198). While these proposals included measures to restructure a seemingly unbalanced ensemble of an extremely large broadcasting institution, NWDR, covering half of the West German territory on the one hand, and extremely small ones, such as RB, serving just one, medium-sized city, on the other, the federal government wanted to get a stake in broadcasting itself. While NWDR dominance was no problem anymore after separation in 1954/5, both mini-corporations, such as RB and SFB and cross-*Länder* institutions remained on the agenda. For example, in the south-west the newly created *Land* of Baden-Württemberg (BW) had one and a half broadcasting corporations: SDR with its headquarters in the capital of Stuttgart was solely within BW-authority and covered half of the state. The other half was served by SWF, whose head office was in Baden-Baden (BW). SWF also served, however, the whole of Rhineland-Palatinate (*Rheinland-Pfalz*). Correspondingly, SWF was a bi-state corporation. Because SWF was broadcasting across *Länder* boundaries – thereby cutting BW into two halves – it was long considered an 'unnatural solution' (Schmücker 1970). According to federal government plans in the 1950s, SWF was to be reorganised fundamentally, bringing regional broadcasting monopolies more in line with *Länder* territories.

The 1950s witnessed several attempts by the Adenauer government in Bonn to regulate broadcasting in Germany. *Länder* governments and broadcasting corporations reacted by proposing alternative federal legislation – not necessarily by a complete refusal. Nevertheless, both *Länder* and broadcasters aimed at fixing arrangements (Fromm 1998: 25) and legal realities in order to deprive the federal government of its rationale to pass framework regulation. ARD corporations began to deepen what had formerly been a loose arrangement, thus making ARD more effective (Diller 1975: 43). In 1959, the *Länder* governments signed the first state treaty, indirectly sanctioning the private law agreement of the ARD corporations of 1950. Moreover, when the broadcasting corporations became aware of legislative proposals by the federal government, to grant authority to the German postal services (*Deutsche Bundespost* (DBP)) in order to provide for fiscal equalisation, using the broadcasting fees they collected (Diller 1975: 42), ARD corporations reacted by passing a fiscal equalisation agreement in 1954 (Thieme 1963). Finally, the international programme of ARD, the *Deutsche Welle*, established in 1953, was given over fully into federal hands in 1960 (Herres and Plog 1989: 27), not in the least, because Adenauer had the stronger argument here: broadcasting abroad affected foreign affairs, which undoubtedly belonged to the federal powers. It can well be argued that the threat by the federal government to regulate broadcasting had been a major force in both enhancing co-operation among public broadcasting corporations within the ARD regime and in making *Länder* governments realise the need to get more involved in broadcasting matters, especially by legally sanctioning ARD proceedings.

Despite this rather indirect and not necessarily intentional impact on *Länder* and ARD, all the regulative efforts of Adenauer remained unsuccessful, partly due to party politics[5], and partly due to the need to assemble a majority in the second chamber (*Bundesrat*), where the *Länder* governments are represented. Giving in on regulatory measures, Adenauer now wanted to establish a federal television network. Since his plans of 1959 to create a public television corporation governed by federal public law, which would have left the making of programmes to private corporations, had failed due to *Bundesrat* disapproval, he simply established a federally dominated company governed by private law, the *Deutschland-Fernsehen GmbH*, which – obeying the letter of the constitution, if not its spirit – did not request Bundesrat approval. However, it became quite obvious that *Deutschland-Fernsehen* was designed to serve as the channel for the federal government, strongly violating the framework order of broadcasting set up by the allies in Germany after 1945. Consequently, several *Länder* filed a suit and brought the case to the BVerfG in Karlsruhe (BVerfGE 12, 205). In the so-called 'First Television Decision' (*Erstes Fernsehurteil*) of 1961, the BVerfG ruled out federal television as being unconstitutional.

The judgement of the BVerfG was a landmark decision and a watershed event for broadcasting in Germany, the first in a series of rulings which have since been compiled into a 'Magna Charta' of German broadcasting (Herres and Plog 1989: 28). It has shaped public (and private, for that matter) broadcasting in Germany, not only because it granted broadcasting authority to the *Länder* (BVerfGE 12, 205 (246)) – only technical aspects of transmission were left to the DBP, hence the federal government – but also because it elevated 'broadcasting independence from the state' (*Staatsferne* or *Staatsfreiheit*) to the level of constitutional law. The rationale provided by the BVerfG is based on Art. 5 of the Basic Law, protecting freedom of speech and the freedom of the press. The court argued that freedom of speech is not only to be considered a fundamental right, protecting individuals against the state, but also a prerequisite for the functioning of democracy. The latter needs 'diversity (or pluralism) of opinions' (*Meinungsvielfalt*), which hence has to be ensured by the state. This paradox of independence from the state (*Staatsfreiheit*) and state responsibility for pluralistic broadcasting (*Rundfunkgewährleistung*) is solved by the court through the given construction of independent, yet state-sponsored public broadcasting services. Even though the state has no editorial say whatsoever in broadcasting (that would infringe on both journalists' fundamental rights and ensuring diversity), it has to give a guarantee for public broadcasting as an institution. From this, it follows that the *Länder* not only have to provide sufficient funding, but also a framework which ensures that all important societal groups have a stake in broadcasting. This latter finding of the court has since consolidated the power of the *Rundfunkräte*. A more formal consequence of the *Staatsfreiheit* principle (Lehment 1996: 55–110) is that the state must not monitor the management of broadcasting corporations in detail (*Fachaufsicht*), but has to restrict monitoring to the safeguarding of the rule of law (*Rechtsaufsicht*).

The decision did not, however, necessarily ban private broadcasting (BVerfGE 12, 205 (262)). It set high standards which had to be met – more or less the same as for public broadcasting – and it ruled out federal efforts. Moreover, the court held that as long as frequency availability is highly limited, (*Länder*) legislators may opt for the then incumbent purely public broadcasting model. Despite several efforts to establish private broadcasting by both *Länder* governments and private players in the years to come, it was not until 1978 that the *Länder* governors (*Ministerpräsidenten*) decided to start the so-called 'cable pilot project' (*Kabelpilotprojekt*), which paved the way for private broadcasting in Germany.

However, as a consequence of the 1961 decision, and just a few days after its pronouncement, the ZDF (*Zweites Deutsches Fernsehen*) was founded by all the *Länder* in a joint effort to establish a second national television channel (Zuck 1999: 1333). Internally organised more or less like ARD member corporations, it was created by an inter-state treaty of all the *Länder* governments. Until 1984, when the *Kabelpilotprojekt* finally started in four selected cities, only three TV channels served the country: two national programmes by ARD and ZDF and the regional programmes by ARD member corporations.

Regulating from inside?

Before looking more thoroughly at who regulates what, we need to face up to the critical question of whether looking at public broadcasting is really an issue for the study of the regulatory state. In fact, one could certainly ignore the public system and focus on the more recent developments in private broadcasting. It is certainly not easy to locate public broadcasting in the regulatory scheme. There are, however, several reasons why I would argue that public broadcasting has to be considered as a case, which, in turn, implies that the 'regulation' of broadcasting, in the way that the concept is used in this study, had already started after the Second World War. First, as argued earlier, public broadcasting corporations have a considerable degree of independence from the state, especially with regard to matters of programme. Even though formally created by a state act (or inter-state treaty), they are but mere agents of the state (Gersdorf 1991: 238). Nevertheless, I do not deny that the fact that public broadcasters do not originally emerge from the *market system* is a problem for using them as a case. In the end, however, it seems undeniable that they adopt strategies of behaviour similar to those displayed by other 'regulated'. That means, we observe a similar form of juxtaposition of state (as a regulator) and public broadcasting corporations (as the regulated).

Second, the state, i.e. the *Länder*, have reserved certain regulatory powers. They are, of course, largely bound by the framework set up by the BVerfG. However, that does not make them fully irrelevant. The regulatory competencies extend to financing (i.e. broadcasting fees and the distribution thereof among public broadcasters), assigning frequencies (which is a matter that concerns private broadcasters as well) and defining certain organisational features of public broadcasting corporations (e.g. the Director versus Board of Directors controversy). In other words, public broadcasting provides diverse forms of regulation, making their study especially interesting.

Third, as will be discussed presently, public broadcasters can be said to be regulated from within. While this seems to sit rather awkwardly with the concept of regulation as developed earlier, the following will illustrate that organisational characteristics of public broadcasting are at least functionally equivalent, if not an exotic institutional specification.

When looking at who regulates what issues, we have to distinguish between programme and organisational issues as well as financial ones. First, *programme decisions* are almost totally internal. As described earlier, while traditionally the director has a powerful position (and that holds for directorial boards as well), the 'supervision' is mainly handed on to the 'broadcasting councils'. There had been plans in the 1940s to construct these councils as legally independent bodies, 'regulatory', so to speak. But in the end, they opted for an incorporated solution. What is crucial, however, is that according to the logic of the public broadcasting system, these councils can be seen as forms of *delegated self-regulation*. They are not simply 'organs' of public broadcasters, but bodies of public, yet state-free, control which is exercised by societal groups. One might object that the broadcasting councils are merely a feature of corporate governance. I would, however, base my claim on the very fact that determining *which* group is to be represented – as well as some general aspects of their functions, such as public versus non-public session – is subject to *Länder* legislation. Thus, their function and their functioning extends beyond what supervisory boards and the like fulfil in private firms. Their *raison d'être* is regulation and in performing this role, they are tied up to the legislator.

Second, while fundamental aspects of regulation are left with the broadcasting councils and the corporations' directorial level, the *Länder* still decide upon certain organisational, financial and technical questions. *Länder* parliaments have installed different organisational arrangements, as argued earlier, and even though they have not been proven to work very much more efficiently (Bethge 1995), the BVerfG has not generally hindered legislators to be innovative. Obviously, the court has not found all the changes described earlier to constitute a threat to 'broadcasting freedom'. This became evident right after the 1961 decision of the BVerfG. I would therefore argue that the succeeding years might be labelled as a period of 'politicisation'. Nevertheless, the institutional arrangement of public broadcasting which has proved to have developed enormous robustness and effective 'co-ordination' and 'co-operation', especially between the two networks, has been successful in helping to fight off political aspirations.

The *Länder*, assured by the BVerfG that they have legislative authority in broadcasting, re-formulated their broadcasting acts and inter-state treaties respectively with regard to both the re-organisation of decision-making and their power within the broadcasting corporations as well as finance. As to the first, party politics became more visible. For one, *Länder* governments changed the law and sent representatives from their parliaments on the broadcasting councils

(Herres and Plog 1989: 26). These efforts to politicise public broadcasting had, however, been slowed down or stopped partly by the courts, and partly by the public. An example illustrating the latter is Art. 111a of the Bavarian constitution (Bethge 1997: 401–402; Maassen 1979).

In 1972, the Bavarian government presented a proposal to reform the BR Act which would have cut the director's power (and enhanced the broadcasting council's rights respectively), provided for more representatives from the Bavarian parliament in the council and, last but not least, allowed for private broadcasting. Mainly due to the rather blatant attempt to politicise broadcasting in Bavaria, the public protested strongly against the proposal and a committee was organised to urge for a referendum. In 1973, the referendum was held and gained a vast majority. The proposition contained a new article 111a to the Bavarian constitution, which first, limits the number of parliamentary representatives in the broadcasting council of BR and second, rules out private broadcasting by stating that broadcasting is a matter of public service and is to be exclusively carried out by public law institutions. The article is still in force and provoked a decision by the Bavarian Constitutional Court (*Bayerischer Verfassungsgerichtshof* (BayVerfGH)) in 1986 (Degenhart 1987), which spectacularly tried to square the circle by legitimising private broadcasting in Bavaria under the umbrella of an organisation established under public law.

Similarly, other *Länder* have had an eye on seats in the broadcasting councils. In the 1970s, worker participation and a certain dislike of monocratic structures became popular, especially with SPD-led governments (Humphreys 1994: 187–190). Consequently, legal reform provided for the replacement of the Director's statute (*Intendantenverfassung*) by a Board of Directors' statute (*Direktoralverfassung*) in a number of broadcasting corporations. Similarly, the number of worker representatives was increased, especially on the board of supervisors which had formerly been highly dominated by broadcasting council members. Another fashion in the 1970s was to make broadcasting council sessions open to the public (Herres and Plog 1989: 31). Despite a widespread neo-conservatism in the 1980s and 1990s some of these features have survived, though in a modified way.

Politicisation as a feature of broadcasting regulation in the period after 1961 can also be identified in the so-called 'NDR crisis' (*NDR-Krise*) of 1978, which lasted until 1980 (ARD 1980: 101–110). NDR is the public broadcasting service of the north, sponsored at that time by three *Länder* (*Schleswig-Holstein*, *Hamburg* and *Niedersachsen*). Due to political differences, there had been a long vacancy for the director's as well as the vice-director's position. Decision-making within the broadcasting council had become almost impossible and the daily business was gridlocked (Herres and Plog 1989: 31–32). In several cases, courts had to decide and do the job instead. Moreover, the CDU governor of *Niedersachsen* developed plans for introducing private broadcasting in his *Land*, asking NDR to cede frequencies. This provoked a major controversy with *Hamburg*, and in the course of this dispute the CDU-led *Länder* of *Schleswig-Holstein* and *Niedersachsen* cancelled the NDR inter-state treaty. NDR and *Hamburg* filed a lawsuit with the BVerwG in Berlin and reached a decision, which held that, first, for formal reasons, the *Niedersachsen* notice was invalid and second, the *Schleswig-Holstein* notice did not terminate NDR as a whole. In view of this judgement, the three started negotiations on a new state treaty and signed up for a more stable arrangement in 1980.

In view of these attempts to gain political control of public broadcasting, networks have reacted by strategies of 'consolidation' and 'co-ordination'. After all, by and large, nothing substantial had changed as far as the organisation of public broadcasting in Germany is concerned. Despite crises, such as the one mentioned above, and numerous attempts to re-structure certain corporations (such as SWF, SDR and SR), ARD proved to be a stable regime. It seems that strong federalism, of which broadcasting is an example, does not necessarily lead to instability of cross-regional arrangements. Rather, strengthened by two other judgements of the BVerfG in 1971 (BVerfGE 31, 314) and 1981 (BVerfGE 57, 295), ARD and ZDF learned to live with the political uncertainties, knowing well that the judiciary is a reliable ally. Despite a certain degree of competition, both networks realised that co-operation is more rewarding than concurrence and hence have been co-ordinating certain aspects of programme making, education and training or technical development since. Even though they faced attempts of 'reverse capture' (i.e. the state as a regulator – the *Länder* – tried to get hold of the regulated – the broadcasting corporations), they succeeded in consolidating their independence from the state as a separate sphere of decision-making.

Finance – limping self-regulation, inter-federal inertia and regulation by expertise

In particular, ARD and ZDF have proved to be able to co-operate quite effectively where common financial interests are concerned. In 1968, ARD and ZDF sued the German postal services (DBP) in order to terminate DBP's 'service' of collecting the broadcasting fees (Schmücker 1973). The postal service had administered licence fee collection since the Weimar Republic and considered it an inalienable constitutional must. However, ARD and ZDF won and set up a joint institution, the *Gebühreneinzugszentrale der öffentlich-rechtlichen Rundfunkanstalten in der Bundesrepublik Deutschland* (GEZ), which started collecting licence fees in 1975. The rationale was not only to become independent from DBP, but also to save costs.

Generally speaking, finance concerns both the level of licence fees as well as their distribution among public broadcasters. As this matter exceeds *Länder* boundaries, it has to be dealt with co-operatively by all *Länder* in inter-state treaties. It is hardly surprising that financial equalisation arrangements have been constantly changing. Since the foundation of ZDF, all licence fee increases had been linked to a new mode of distribution among ARD members and ZDF. Interestingly, both distribution and equalisation have since been alternately determined by inter-state treaty (of all *Länder*) or by agreement among the broadcasting corporations (Lehment 1996: 15). The latter has been the case in particular when *Länder* governments were unable to reach agreement. *Self-co-ordination* among ARD members has, of course, never been easy when it comes to finance. Both directors and council representatives did, however, prove capable of finding compromises in order to avoid unrequested political solutions, which might have endangered the system as a whole.

Setting licence fees has been extremely problematic since ARD and ZDF have to share, bringing in a new criterion in addition to the formerly exclusive principle of territory. But there is also a more fundamental problem with regard to the logic of action: On the one hand, politicians have always had few incentives to follow the wishes of ARD and ZDF (which, of course, regularly asked for higher funding), because voters will dislike higher broadcasting fees, and moreover, politicians cannot even dispose of these funds. On the other hand, the courts, including BVerfG, have explicitly ruled that politics and the state must not even indirectly control programme making (Gersdorf 1991: 309–371) by using their power to set licence fee rates (Fromm 1998: 44). Moreover, financing must not only be sufficient to keep the *status quo*, but also to allow for development (*Bestands- und Entwicklungsgarantie*). The problem was solved in 1975 by setting up a commission on broadcasting fees, the *Kommission zur Ermittlung des Finanzbedarfs der Rundfunkanstalten* (KEF), to report and recommend on licence fee increases. The KEF used to include government (or parliamentary) representatives well into the 1990s, when BVerfG ruled out any political representation as a violation of the *Staatsferne* principle (BVerfGE 90, 60). Since then, mainly experts from academia and the courts of auditors study ARD and ZDF data and their proposals for fee increases in order to make suggestions to the *Länder* governments. The latter have shown a tendency to follow KEF recommendations. *Länder* governments have thus been proven to adopt a strategy of *de facto expert regulation*. Accepting KEF findings is partly due to the logic of co-operative federalism. Where the consent of 16 prime ministers has to be found, the expert's proposal has a certain advantage to get through unchanged as the 'neutral' compromise. Moreover, KEF reports display a considerable degree of criticism of ARD and ZDF's wishes for more funding. Of course, it is the commission's implied task to cut down on public broadcasters' demands. However, the experts now left alone in the KEF evidently do not try to assume the image of an ally of public broadcasting.

Even though parliaments have to ratify the inter-state treaties, *Länder* governments try out ways to transfer power from the legislature to themselves. A revealing example is § 29 I of the ZDF-*Staatsvertrag*, which regulates the ZDF share (30 per cent) of the broadcasting fees. However, sentence two stipulates that the *Länder* governors (sic!) can by means of agreement (*Vereinbarung*) change the percentage (Bethge 1995: 115–116). It should be here re-emphasised that distribution of fees among public broadcasters, including the financial equalisation arrangement, has been a political issue since ZDF joined the group of public broadcasting corporations. The relative degree of inertia in this field is probably best explained by reference to the above-mentioned logic of co-operative federalism.

Frequency, cable and satellite assignments – a point of regulatory intersection

Finally, the assignment of *frequencies* constitutes a special problem of regulating public broadcasting. While private corporations receive their assignments from the LMAs, the *Länder* have adopted very different approaches to deal with this matter for public broadcasters (Gersdorf 1991: 279–308). At the heart of this problem is the question of how to assign new frequencies to public and private corporations in view of, first, the principle of 'independence from the state' (*Staatsfreiheit*) and second, the 'basic supply' doctrine (*Grundversorgung*) as set up by the BVerfG: ARD and ZDF have to be given a guarantee to develop and provide the 'basic supply'; private broadcasters need frequencies (terrestrial, cable and satellite) to develop their business (making use of their fundamental rights in Art. 5 Basic Law).

At first, all the *Länder* had kept their hands off old frequencies, already used by ARD and ZDF. In addition to this unanimous consent, governments had been creative (Eberle 1989). Four groups can be distinguished. First, assignment by *parliament*. According to the government's proposal, parliament decides whether new terrestrial frequencies are assigned either to the LMA or to public broadcasting. Second, assignment by *government*. Procedures are similar to the first category, except that parliament does not participate. Third, assignment by *LMAs*. LMAs put forward a plan of how the frequencies available can be distributed among public and private broadcasters. Fourth, informal assignment by *state chancelleries*. Here the law states that the LMA in the respective *Land* should assign only those frequencies which it has previously 'received' for that purpose. It is, however, left open *how* the frequencies for the LMA (hence private broadcasters) and how frequencies for public broadcasting are distributed in the first place. In practice this decision is made by the state chancelleries who have enormous discretion since there is no legal basis governing the regulation of frequencies. Beside these institutional features, *Länder* have adopted provisions in their legal arrangements, granting either public or private broadcasters a certain prerogative. Even the *Rundfunkstaatsvertrag* for all the *Länder* has been interpreted as having given preferential treatment to private broadcasters regarding new frequencies.

The position is quite different for *cable* assignments. Almost all *Länder* have passed laws providing for detailed regulation on cable priority groups. According to these provisions, there is hardly any room for discretion. The executive authority is, however, vested in the LMAs. With regard to public broadcasting, there is no regulatory room for manouevre, as the public system ranks among the first to be assigned on cable (Gersdorf 1991: 296–298).

Finally, the assignment of satellite channels is governed by different regulatory regimes. First, where direct-broadcasting satellites operate under German law (operated by the DBP), the *Länder* had to act together. Second, where the DBP had rented channels, such as on ECS1, the *Länder* governors had to allocate them, too. Third, broadcasters simply leased transponders on foreign satellites, such as on Luxembourg's Astra (Humphreys 1994: 271).

Generally speaking, the new *dual broadcasting order* has also brought about some changes in the institutional arrangements for the regulation of public broadcasting. While matters of programme decisions have been left with the broadcasting councils, which serve as a form of 'delegated self-regulatory institution' inside the regulated, and while matters of finance have remained an issue of co-operative federalism, regulated effectively by the recommendations of an independent expert commission, the assignment of frequencies has been proven to need institutional change. Before private broadcasters were admitted, the frequencies available were assigned on a territorial basis. The German postal services would simply execute an equal distribution doctrine among public broadcasters. However, since private corporations concur, an alternative solution, beyond that of territory, had to be found. It included quite different institutional arrangements, varying from *Land* to *Land*. It becomes obvious that there was a certain political desire to keep some control within government – even if it was just to carefully fix priorities in favour of private or public broadcasting. The BVerfG interfered, of course, in the case of *Baden-Württemberg*, making it clear that the public system may not be slowly worn away. Be that as it may, public broadcasting had been partly dragged out of its regulatory 'ivory tower', even though the general approach of 'regulating from within' has not been abandoned.

Private broadcasting

The emergence of private broadcasting and the *dual order* respectively was not due to some higher logic of general liberalisation, but came about as a result of three developments in particular. First, technological progress regarding both the development of cable technology as well as the provision of new frequencies allowed for additional broadcasters. Second, however, this does not provide enough reasons why *private* broadcasting was given a chance. I would argue that *ideology* and a certain party-political bias, especially on the part of the CDU/CSU parties, have promoted the rise of private broadcasting. Governments have understood that private broadcasting might allow more discretion in the shaping of broadcasting than the public corporations had allowed in the past. Third, the BVerfG pointed to the individual right to start a broadcasting business once the scarcity of frequencies had been reduced. Furthermore, the court developed a range of mostly institutional requirements regarding the state regulation of private broadcasting, effectively separating once more the sphere of making programmes from statal-political influence. This approach resulted in an arrangement somewhat similar to public broadcasting, except that it is 'external'. Consequently, a similarity of institutional design resulted in a similarity in attempts to politicise it.

Ideological regulation versus co-operative regulation – a problem of German federalism

As early as 1975, the *Kommission für den Ausbau des technischen Kommunikationssystems* (KtK), set up a year earlier, reported its assessment of the technological developments in communications. Among its recommendations was a pilot project to test cable TV and radio in selected areas. In 1978 the governors in the *Länder* decided to set up a 'pilot cable project' (*Kabelpilotprojekt*) in certain urban areas and to re-consider the admission of private broadcasting afterwards. There had, of course, been certain preferences to admit private broadcasting right away – the above-mentioned 'NDR crisis' partly escalated due to them – and these tendencies were stronger in CDU-led *Länder* than in SPD-governed ones. The CDU had always felt that public broadcasting was rather 'leftist' and some had been hoping for a more conservative tenor in private TV and radio. For SPD governments it was clear that cable technology should not be an exclusive carrier for private broadcasting (e.g., Niewiarra 1989: 18). Both the Conservatives and the Social Democrats knew, however, that technological innovations (and cable promised to be that) had to be used and maintained publicly.

It needed about six years to finally come up with the project. This extremely long period of time is said to have been entirely due to German federalism

(Neupert 1997: 379). Four urban areas were finally selected: Ludwigshafen/Mannheim, München, Dortmund and Berlin. Planning for the completion of the project was almost completely decentralised, each *Land* doing its work locally. However, in the so-called *Kronberger Beschluß* the *Länder* governors agreed to provide common funding for these selected test areas (DLM 1988: 6). As was agreed in 1982, funding should come from the so-called *Kabelgroschen*, i.e. an additional licence fee set on top of broadcasting fees. This has been kept and still finances private broadcasting regulation today (Merznicht 1992).

While the projects were being set up, the *Länder* governments passed new laws on broadcasting, more or less leaving room for private TV and radio corporations to gain a foothold. Thus, before any substantial results from the projects could be assessed, it was clear that private broadcasting was now a fact in Germany (Humphreys 1994: 229–230). One day after transmission on cable started in Ludwigshafen, RTL-Plus, a TV channel from CLT in Luxembourg, began to broadcast across the boarder by using conventional, terrestrial transmission technology. By broadcasting from abroad, CLT opened politicians' eyes to the reality of a potentially Europeanised broadcasting market, which threatened to make national regulation partially obsolete (Fromm 1998: 32). The development of satellite technology heightened the problem.

In the very same year, 1984, the *Länder* governments had striven for an inter-state treaty (Humphreys 1994: 250–252) in order to co-ordinate the development of private broadcasting in Germany. But a compromise was not reached until 1987 in the first 'Inter-State Broadcasting Treaty' (*Rundfunkstaatsvertrag*). The discussion was characterised by fundamental gaps regarding what effects private TV and radio would have on the country. The debate was reminiscent of religious wars (Neupert 1997: 379). The *Länder* governments had in part thought about signing inter-state treaties with only those *Länder* which had similar ideas on the balance of private and public broadcasting. While *Teilstaatsverträge* are an unproblematic instrument where technically mandated, they were generally ruled out by the BVerfG as a means to regulate 'essential matters' in 1986 (Halefeldt 1989: 37). Governments had, in part, simply passed their own laws (Fromm 1998: 32). Although *Baden-Württemberg* was the first to propose a new bill, it was *Niedersachsen* who was the very first to pass a bill (*Landesrundfunkgesetz* (LRG Nds.)) in May 1984 and thus ushered in a new series of BVerfG decisions.

After it was clear that private broadcasting was to become a reality, the *Länder* had to cope with three central questions in particular. First, what institutional structures should be set up to be entrusted with admitting and monitoring private broadcasting? Second, how should tasks of cross-*Länder* relevance, especially national programmes, be tackled? And third, what role should public broadcasting be assigned in the new regulatory arrangement?

The *Länder* opted for the so-called dual broadcasting system (*Duale Rundfunkordnung*), containing both a public broadcasting system, still supported by the state and based on incorporated semi-self regulation, and a private broadcasting system, governed by an institutional regulatory regime, almost completely separate. It does not by any means completely follow market logic.

Landesmedienanstalten as independent regulatory agencies

Despite the highly decentralised, if not chaotic beginning, the new regulatory regimes established are quite similar throughout the *Länder*. What had been partly incorporated into public broadcasting services has been set up as the prototype of an *independent regulatory agency* in the case of private broadcasters (Wagner 1990). The 'State Media Agencies' *Landesmedienanstalten* (LMAs) have basically been given full regulatory authority over private corporations. They also decide upon the assignment of channels on local or regional cable networks. Insofar, they affect public broadcasting as well. Due to the BVerfG doctrine of 'independence from the state', the LMAs have been designed merely as a 'fourth branch', located somewhere outside the executive and legislature, enjoying a legal status which grants them autonomy (Lammek 1997: 21). That is not self-evident. After all, LMAs are not broadcasting corporations; their task lies in the supervision and monitoring thereof, in order to ensure a certain degree of 'pluralism' in private broadcasting. The courts as well as scholarly opinion have found it necessary to grant LMAs more or less the same status as public broadcasting corporations. What ARD and ZDF have incorporated in their 'broadcasting councils' – and which, for obvious reasons, commercial TV and radio does not wish to create voluntarily – had to be 'imitated' in the regulatory agency. In other words, what had been regulated internally in public broadcasting, had become a matter of 'external' regulation for private broadcasting.

The *Bayerische Landeszentrale für Neue Medien* (BLM) is special insofar as it is not only a regulatory institution, but also – due to Art. 111a of the Bavarian constitution – the legal organiser (*Veranstalter*) of private broadcasting. In reality, differences to the other *Länder* are marginal, except for a higher degree of politicising (Keidel 1993). It seems, however, that this rather strange construction of allowing private broadcasting under the umbrella of public law has provoked more juridical interference than the usual regulator-regulated-arrangement elsewhere. It might be worth noting here in this context that, after German unification, the new *Länder* in the east mainly imitated their Western neighbours, by referring to particular models of those *Länder* in particular, with whom they were in any case co-operating on an administrative level (Schuler-Harms 1992).

Generally speaking, similarities between LMAs and public broadcasters are striking. First, both are created on the *Land* level. Second, both have been given the same legal form (a 'self-administered corporation governed by public law' – *selbständige Anstalt des öffentlichen Rechts*). They are subject only to limited state supervision (Varenhold 1992: 115), which is restricted to the safeguarding of the rule of law (*Rechtsaufsicht*). Third, like public broadcasters LMAs receive part of the licence fee revenue. Fourth, LMAs, as well as public broadcasting corporations, have an executive and a pluralistic 'legislative' organ; the latter is in both cases made up of representatives from 'socially significant groups' (Schuler-Harms 1995: 33). The executive organ consists, however, either of a board of directors or of a monocratic director. The distribution of competencies between executive and pluralistic 'legislature' is about the same as in public broadcasting corporations: the pluralistic organ decides on fundamentals and the board of directors is the executor.

Nevertheless, the executive body is predominant, owing to a range of institutional and procedural reasons. While the director's position is a permanent and well-paid public office, representatives in the pluralistic 'legislative' body have no such privilege. They convene occasionally, in order to decide upon issues prepared by the executive and its staff. Accordingly, members of the 'legislature' lack detailed knowledge, information about alternatives and – as they are not usually experts on broadcasting – expertise (Hellstern and Reese 1989: 18–20). On the other hand, it is the executives who have the means to gather information informally and to negotiate. Formal action taken by the LMA is usually preceded by informal talks with the regulated, be they on a general level or specifically against a broadcaster's non-compliance (Lammek 1997: 30). The executive is addressee for any inquiries on behalf of the regulated (Wagner 1990: 116) and moreover, it takes over all controlling functions, supervising private programmes, giving notice in case of violation and, if necessary, preparing an enforced sanction for the 'legislature' to decide (Gersdorf 1991: 165). The high standard of 'jurisprudence' provides the legally trained management and staff of the LMAs with a natural advantage (Ziethen 1989: 59–161). In short, executive predominance is another similiarity between LMAs and public broadcasting corporations. However, the councils fulfil a specific and important function, i.e. generating societal legitimacy. Where a relatively broad selection of societal forces and groups backs programme decisions of journalists and the director in the case of public broadcasting, or a general regulatory policy regarding private broadcasters in the case of the LMAs, decision-makers can usually be sure that harsh criticism is largely banned, thereby increasing societal acceptance. Furthermore, such organs of societal representation serve to some extent more informally as a 'self-check' for decision-makers in the executive.

Politicisation is an important issue with regard to both executive and legislative bodies, and it seems even stronger than in public broadcasting. First, the director's position is filled according to political decision-making. They are nominated by the respective *Land* government and elected by parliament. In *Baden-Württemberg*, for instance, a two-thirds majority in parliament (*Landtag*) is necessary, modelled in accordance with the method of election of judges to the BVerfG. Even though the quorum seems to prevent party politics, it is but a mechanism to extend party politics over the boundaries of a coalition government. The *lex Beerstecher*, which was part of the 1994/5 reform of the *Baden-Württemberg* Media Act (LMG BW), is a telling example of blatant political influence.

In 1994, vice-president Klaus Haischer of the *Landesanstalt für Kommunikation* (LfK), the LMA in *Baden-Württemberg*, was to be replaced by a nominee of the SPD, *Beerstecher*. At that time, a grand coalition of CDU and SPD governed the state of *Baden-Württemberg*. After the electoral defeat of Beerstecher, the government introduced an amendment to the LMG BW, changing § 66 III, effectively abandoning the two-thirds majority requirement. There was still, however, another formal problem. As a member of the board of management of the *Landeskreditbank*, a state-owned financial agency exercising control over public subsidies, Beerstecher's nomination violated the 'incompatibility doctrine' of § 67 I (old version) LMG BW. Neither Beerstecher nor his party were willing to abandon that position. Thus, in 1995 § 67 I was amended, effectively lifting the incompatibility restriction. Shortly after the legislative hurdles were removed, Beerstecher was elected vice-president by a simple majority vote. The CDU–SPD government did not even try to hush up the party-political background in its justification of the amendment, referring to 'political balance' in the LfK board of directors. While the original argument of the government for the 1985 Media Act was strongly in favour of incompatibility – and the significant reforms of 1987 and 1991 had not seen any new consideration of the issue – the government seemed to have changed its mind at the very moment a political bargain was to be made. *Lex Beerstecher* has, of course, provoked major criticism in scholarly contributions (e.g., Kirschnek 1998: 156–158).

The *lex Beerstecher* affair is a rather extreme case, but political appointments are no exception. Looking at who became director, or member of the board, one will find no experts from academia or broadcasting, but former (or current) political advisers to governors or governments. Some of them, like Beerstecher, had a political career in parliament before their appointment.

Similarly, the pluralistic 'legislative' body, which has different names in the *Länder* laws, is politically influenced insofar as the law defines the groups, which are permitted to send representatives. What holds for the broadcasting councils in public broadcasting corporations is equally valid for LMAs. In many cases, it is well known which group considers itself close to which party. Thus, the selection of groups is carefully crafted, striving once more for 'political balance' (Hellstern and Reese 1989: 12–14). However, the arrangement has to be qualified as *co-operative*, institutionalising once more a form of judicially forced control by societal groups. It might be understood as a societally delegated self-regulatory regime, in which the regulated, i.e. private broadcasting corporations, are *not* represented.

A question to be tackled separately from the representation aspect is the problem of 'capture'. 'Capture' does not necessarily assume personal representation within the regulator. Rather, it refers to the fact that the regulators do what the regulated want. When analysing publications from the LMAs, it becomes obvious that, for instance, the 'LMAs' Directors' Conference' (DLM) advocates several positions held by private broadcasters (Kleinsteuber 1993: 43), e.g. a fast distribution of frequencies or restrictions on advertisements in public broadcasting. Moreover, the big media groups, which operate the major broadcasting stations, usually receive the most favourable frequencies (Kaiser 1989). What is even more striking is that Hellstern and Reese (1989: 33–34) have found LMAs in CDU-governed *Länder* to favour broadcasters of the *Springer/Kirch* group, while LMAs in SPD-governed *Länder* prefer broadcasting corporations of the *Bertelsmann* group. That might indicate that 'capture' extends either to matters of ideology or to party-political connections beyond the LMA itself. However these observations might also lead to the conclusion that we face a classical form of 'capture'. It has not necessarily so much to do with personal intermingling – which is hard to prove anyway – but with the identity of interests of the regulated and the regulators. That is why LMAs seem to consider themselves advocates of private broadcasting. Party politics enter in on a second level, where different treatment regarding the regulated is observable. Whatever the causes for this might be, it proves once more a distinct criticism of the 'capture theory', that is, traditionally not enough attention has been paid to differences between (and thus different treatments of) 'the regulated'.

Regulation by inter-federal co-operation

Finally, the institutional arrangement governing private broadcasting regulation shows a feature almost necessarily built into the logic of decentralised broadcasting regulation –. co-operation among LMAs. Co-operation is necessitated by the incongruence of *Länder* authority in broadcasting on the one hand and broadcasting corporations' behaviour on the other. That is, most programmes are not regional, but national. However, there is no national agency to regulate such programmes. Therefore, the LMAs had to find a way to handle this problem, as well as a range of additional issues. The co-operative regime, which had been sanctioned and harmonised in the 1991 *Rundfunkstaatsvertrag*, is built on the 'concentration principle'. This means that the LMA, which has licensed a broadcasting programme first, remains responsible. On the other hand, programmes admitted in one *Land*, must be admitted in all others as well. Therefore, broadcasters will try to have their programme licensed by just one LMA and will then apply for transmission into the rest of the country. Due to decentralised decision-making, it became necessary to harmonise standards with regard to both licensing and supervision; moreover, enforcement mechanisms had to be unified as well. All this was, however, rather difficult, as a certain *Standortwettbewerb* (competition for broadcasting investments) had set in, which threatened to lead to a 'race to the bottom'.

Co-operation between LMAs developed not unlike ARD in the 1950s. It started as a self-regulatory regime, whose legality was quite uncertain for a while until it received political backing in 1991 by the new *Rundfunkstaatsvertrag*. Nevertheless, there are different levels of harmonisation, depending on whether the issue is 'licensing' or 'supervision'. Regional distinction has not been completely abandoned with regard to 'licensing'. The *Rundfunkstaatsvertrag* has not unified this procedure (§ 30 I RfStV), which in turn means that each LMA follows its respective criteria as defined by law or internal statute. However, the inter-state treaty stipulates that procedures shall be 'adjusted' to each other (*Abstimmungsverfahren*). The letter of the law is not exact, generating a range of different interpretations of what 'adjustment' implies.

Nevertheless, maybe because of the uncertain nature and extent of the 'adjustment provision', the LMAs have deepened co-operation on the institutional level. As early as 1985, LMA directors started to meet informally and they kept this forum as the 'LMAs' Directors' Conference' (*Direktorenkonferenz der Landesmedienanstalten* (DLM)). It has been integrated into the new 'Working Group of State Media Agencies in the Federal Republic of Germany' (*Arbeitsgemeinschaft der Landesmedienanstalten in der Bundesrepublik Deutschland*) in 1994. A main competence is the *Abstimmungsverfahren* of §30 *Rundfunkstaatsvertrag*. Despite its rational image, the DLM has proved to be not as harmonious as it would seem. Rather, directors have not even drawn back from suing each other (e.g., BayVerwGH decision of 19 June 1995, 25 B 94.3762). Beside the DLM, it has put two further levels under its roof: the 'Joint Conference' (*Gesamtkonferenz*) and the 'Conference of Council Presidents' (*Gremienvorsitzendenkonferenz*). Finally, there are several task forces (*Gemeinsame Stellen*), which work on specific issues and prepare decisions. They are not merely executive bodies, but round-tables, including representatives from the LMAs. The task forces are, however, partly staffed with experts providing detailed information and expertise, representing a form of self-co-ordination. Successive *Rundfunkstaatsverträge* since 1987 have regularly incorporated these institutions and sanctioned them under public law.

Formally a 'paper tiger', task forces have ways to draw attention to their decisions. For instance, when an LMA violates common guidelines (such as the guidelines on commercials (*Werberichtlinien*) for the *Arbeitsgemeinschaft*), the respective task force (e.g. *Gemeinsame Stelle Werbung*) puts this item on its agenda and passes a case-specific 'recommendation'. If the LMA in question refuses to follow the 'recommendation' of the task force, the issue will be brought to the DLM. At this level, the respective LMA director will be confronted with the violation. Thus, the task force serves as a 'catalyst' to higher levels, where non-compliance within the *Arbeitsgemeinschaft* is more difficult to justify.

Neither one of the conferences has the right to pass binding norms; their decisions are mere 'recommendations'. So far, even the relatively strong DLM has not succeeded in drawing larger competencies. What is interesting, however, is that LMAs respect the normative effect of these 'recommendations', which can be seen when analysing LMAs' decisions. Whenever LMAs deviate from general conference 'recommendations' in concrete decisions, they specifically justify this 'breaking of the rules'. The high degree of normativity might be partly explained by the fact that decisions by these organs need a three-quarters quorum to be passed. Decisions with regard to common guidelines or financial contributions need unanimous consent.

Task forces are certainly under-researched in social science. However, what seems interesting from an institutional point of view is the logic of participants' behaviour therein. Due to the enormous need to agree on common principles, the number of meetings has increased. This represents a certain challenge for smaller LMAs: fewer people to prepare meetings means in practice a more 're-active' approach as opposed to the 'pro-active' behaviour of larger agencies. The latter have the staff to prepare papers and, to some extent, dominate the discourse. This might not always be disadvantageous for the 're-active' LMAs, but it slowly contributes to the building up of a reputation for expertise on behalf of the larger agencies. Moreover, a certain bias in favour of the latter is undeniable even if it is just with regard to the issues dealt with. In view of this reasoning, it seems hardly surprising that there is some co-relation between the size of LMA and the relative importance of the respective region as a site for investment by private broadcasting and TV in particular.

The 1997 *Rundfunkstaatsvertrag* has, in part, changed the original (and self-disciplined) organisation of LMA co-operation in force since 1994. In particular, two new institutions were created by the inter-state treaty, which partially supersede the self-made regime of the LMAs; first, the so-called 'Commission on Investigation about Media Concentration' (*Kommission zur Ermittlung der Konzentration im Medienbereich*) (KEK), based in Potsdam, and second, the 'Conference of Directors of the State Media Agencies' (*Konferenz der Direktoren der Landesmedienanstalten*) (KDLM). While the first is an expert commission, consisting of six experts on broadcasting and competition law, appointed by the governors by mutual consent for a five-year period, the latter is identical to the DLM, except for one aspect: KDLM decisions are final and binding.

Among the many problems which had shown up and needed to be remedied is the process of concentration within the media. As in other sectors, firms have merged and formed groups. Since the late 1980s, there are only two media groups, *Bertelsmann* and *Springer/Kirch*, which dominate private TV. Despite a variety of channels, a classic duopoly has emerged in the private television market, ultimately endangering diversity in programming. The BVerfG had just lowered the standards for private broadcasting compared to public broadcasting, but not completely abandoned the diversity principle in private broadcasting, so the LMAs had to react by supervising and controlling the process of concentration, especially with regard to its impact on programme diversity. The task force 'diversity' (*Gemeinsame Stelle für Vielfaltsicherung*), founded in 1993 by the LMAs and dealing with this matter, was largely functionally replaced by the KEK in 1997 (Neupert 1997: 378). The KEK could perhaps be considered an *inter-federal independent regulatory commission*, whose task it is to enforce the new 'market share model' (*Marktanteilsmodell*) of the 1997 *Rundfunkstaatsvertrag*. According to this model, private broadcasting suppliers may offer as many programmes as they wish, unless they have reached a market share of 30 per cent or above (§ 26 II RfStV (1997)). If their share exceeds this benchmark, no new programme will be admitted. Although the respective LMA remains formally in charge of supervising 'diversity', the KEK now has the final word with regard to evaluating specific cases. Any application of private broadcasters must be passed on to the KEK by the respective LMA, which considers the case and makes a binding decision by a simple majority vote (§ 37 I RfStV (1997)). If the LMA responsible for the application does not accept the KEK's statement, it can refer the decision to the KDLM (Kreile 1997). Only the KDLM can override the KEK decision by a three-quarters majority, effectively replacing the latter by a new one. By creating a *supra-regional* institutional arrangement, the *Länder* have once more shown that they remain active at times when joint action is needed to overcome dysfunctions of the rules made by the LMAs themselves.

It should be added here, however, that the KEK does not replace the 'Federal Cartel Office' (*Bundeskartellamt* (BKartA)) and its powers in competition policy. The BKartA simply acts within a different legal sphere. It operates under a federal law, the Cartel Act (*Gesetz gegen Wettbewerbsbeschränkungen* (GWB)). The standards provided by the law, as woolly and imprecise as they might be, are economic. Even though not necessarily concerned with maximum economic efficiency in the respective markets, the BKartA does not consider aspects alien to economics, such as 'pluralism'. Thus, the 'dominance' to be controlled and fought against by the BKartA is different from the 'dominance' which the KEK supervises. Even though there is a certain dysfunctionality and hence discomfort due to the co-existence of these two spheres of regulatory control (as seen in the more 'economic' sectors such as telecommunications), both are able to work efficiently but quite separate from each other.

Whether KEK and KDLM, set up as institutions with an inter-state treaty legal foundation, will ring in a new era of organisational change on an inter-federal level, remains to be seen. Ideas had been put forward to create an All-State Media Agency ((*gemeinsame*) *Ländermedienanstalt*) to centralise private broadcasting regulation in just one institution of all the *Länder* joined together. However, whether *Länder* governments are prepared to sacrifice regionalised control over broadcasting for the good of a more effective regulatory regime, is more than questionable.

As reported by a top-ranking executive, KEK should not be overrated as regards its future effectiveness. First, the expertise had not really increased, because the 1993 task force was equally as competent regarding the subject matter. The creation of the KEK in the 1997 state treaty had come about because of the judicial conflict between two LMAs regarding the admission of DSF which effectively undermined, to some extent, the trustworthiness of all LMAs. Second, the composition of the KEK has its problems, because some of its members display a certain conflict of interests; on the one hand, they are supposed to monitor critically the development of concentration in the media sector. On the other hand, they serve as attornies-at-law or expert witnesses for precisely these same 'regulated'. Third and finally, the state treaty simply sanctioned the *status quo* of concentration. In a way, the approach is not unlike the 1935 Energy Law (EnWG), which transformed into public law a market structure built up by private players.

In short, the institutional arrangement of public and private broadcasting regulation is deeply divided into two regimes. However, substantial regulatory powers have been vested in bodies, which consist of societal representatives. With regard to private broadcasting regulation the *Länder* show an increasing tendency to build inter-federal institutions (or to create an appropriate common legal foundation for them) as well as expert commissions. The latest example for both is that the KEK should investigate the concentration processes in the media, which is not only an economic problem (that comes under the authority of the Federal Cartel Office), but is also a challenge to the diversity and pluralism of opinions (*Meinungsvielfalt*). The rationale for both the institutionalisation of co-ordinated policy-making and the reliance on experts is twofold. First, broadcasting problems reach beyond the boundaries of the *Länder*, rendering particularism almost impossible with regard to many essential issues. Second, the subject matter involves a demand for extensive knowledge as well as specific expertise, which the LMAs' management does not always provide satisfactorily. Despite their formal independence – making them similar to public broadcasting in some, especially institutional, aspects – the degree of politicisation is still glaringly bad. But there is hope: as in other independent regulatory agencies, such as the *Bundesbank*, political appointments or party-political bias in choosing societal groups to be represented, have often been seen to lose power, when the nominees take up their post. The degree of 'classical' capture, identifiable in LMAs' publications, might indicate that new loyalities and rationales for individual action within organisations emerge after taking up office.

A double-standard regime?

The institutional prerequisites for public and private broadcasting regulation are very different, even though the respective bodies have, surprisingly or not, taken similar paths with regard to self co-ordination. The 'double-standard' objection comes in, however, at another point. While public broadcasters seemingly have an institutional privilege, i.e. delegated self-regulation by incorporated bodies, private corporations are fully dependent on an external regulatory agency. Moreover, due to decentralised structures, private corporations have to rely on the will of the LMAs to co-operate in order to avoid multiple licensing and supervision. The latter had been acknowledged by the LMAs quite early, but, as some cases brought before the courts illustrate (Lammek 1997: 181–183), single LMAs have time and again used the scope for independence, left by the self co-ordinating regime, to break out. This has certainly been a constant source of instability for private broadcasters.

While the two spheres of regulation work differently, the 'double-standard' argument seems exaggerated. First of all, a lot of problems faced by private broadcasters originate from their specific situation; public broadcasting corporations do not need to apply for a licence (because they are already permitted to broadcast). That is a historical, but not necessarily an institutional advantage. Second, supervision of programme matters, which is internalised in public broadcasting, is certainly comparable to supervision by the pluralistic 'legislative' bodies of the LMAs. After all, the latter had been modelled after the broadcasting councils in the public broadcasting corporations. Third, both public and private broadcasting, have to face the *Länder* as a source of regulation, which works time and again. Institutionally spoken, the differences are not as substantial – with regard to their effect on the regulated – as one might assume in the first place. However, with regard to regulatory instruments and modes used by these regulatory agents, which is the subject of the next section, the double-standard objection might well hold true.

The 'Double-Standard' argument holds true in any case, however, regarding judicial decisions of the BVerfG. At the centre of the court's findings has always been the dictum to protect public broadcasting as a prerequisite for admitting private broadcasters (Bethge 1997: 393–396). This logic sounds strange, but it follows from the court's belief in the essential importance of broadcasting (and the opinions presented therein) for democratic sustainability. Only public broadcasting, state-sponsored yet independent from government, can ensure diversity and thus provide for the 'basic supply' (*Grundversorgung*) of TV and radio. Private broadcasters have, of course, all their rights, especially with regard to the freedom of speech. At the same time, the LMAs are obliged to make sure that certain minimum standards of journalistic fairness are met. Nevertheless, in the court's tenor, only public broadcasting is regarded as the reliable guarantor of diversity, quality and a sense of responsibility to society. Hence, it must not be excluded from participation in future technology and has a right to adequate growth (Fromm 1998: 34). Some governments, such as *Baden-Württemberg* had tried in the 1980s to limit the future development of public broadcasting by excluding it from the assignment of new frequencies (e.g., BVerfGE 87, 181). The government failed in the court. ARD and ZDF succeeded in establishing several satellite programmes, too, now focusing on special interests (e.g. culture in *3SAT*) and groups (e.g. a children's channel). *Länder* governments had to learn that public broadcasting is specifically protected by the BVerfG and any attempt to directly or indirectly limit its scope of action would result in juridical failure. On the other hand, public broadcasting corporations have learned to use the BVerfG as a resource: it became a political weapon to threaten government, if anything goes through parliament that public broadcasters did not like. It is hardly surprising that conservative governments and their philosophy of deregulation, bringing in private broadcasting, had been more under fire from public broadcasters than SPD governments with a more favourable attitude towards the public system.

d) Compliance: protecting broadcasting against the enemy within

Not only are the two regulatory spheres institutionally organised separately, but also the regulators therein apply specific mechanisms and instruments to make broadcasters comply with the regulatory goals.

Here, the public broadcasting system displays all the advantages of a *separate* and *incumbent* regulatory arrangement, which is partly internalised. Public broadcasters are, as 'incumbents', excluded from several regulatory tasks necessary for newcomers. They do not need to be licensed, they already have frequencies to use and they are excluded from any external 'diversity' considerations, potentially leading to the investigation of media concentration. Pluralism is ensured by incorporated broadcasting councils, which in turn makes the very 'act' of the regulatory safeguarding of 'diversity' a matter of internal discussion and bargaining. The directors of both the ARD and ZDF corporations enjoy a struc-

Federalism and sub-national regionalism have been crucial factors in the years after the Second World War and the creation of the incumbent banking regime in 1961. The *Länder* have fought hard to keep the institutional side of banking regulation, but the Federal Constitutional Court decided in favour of the federal level. The 'compromise' offered by the federal government was a relatively weak office in Berlin, substantially unable to fulfil the regulatory tasks alone. It had to rely on both *delegation* of regulatory power to semi-private institutions, such as auditors and auditing associations to supervise banking accounting annually, and close *co-operation* with the *Bundesbank*. As it is clear that the future banking regime will be more 'integrative', comprising financial services as a whole, this institutional co-operation of two federal agencies is more likely than ever to turn into rivalry.

In an ever more globalised financial market, policy-learning becomes an administrative must for the regulator vis-à-vis goals and instruments; if in Basle, for example, one national regulator pursues a distinct protectionist strategy, all others are forced to imitate such behaviour. Otherwise, they run the risk of pushing their national industries into a more disadvantageous position. And even apart from such tactical reasoning, learning from experiences with new instruments, such as risk management techniques, of both the regulators and the regulated abroad is a simple necessity to meet the expectations of the national banking business. However, contrary to what may be expected from some theoretical literature, there is no general 'run to the bottom'. Rather, regulatory density and complexity increases, even though there is a trend to more individualisation, flexibility and fewer 'quantitative rules'. After all, it is in the interest of the regulator, the regulated and society to apply the suitable regulatory modes to ensure systemic stability without endangering national competitiveness (by high costs provoked by unduly rigid rules).

Even though the notion of a re-assessment on behalf of the regulated might not be the precise concept, the regulators both in Germany and internationally are more concerned about the needs (or wishes) of their national banking sectors today than they were in the past. Financial markets are not only an important economic factor in all advanced industrial countries, but represent a crucial politico-economic characteristic in Germany in particular. Banks are traditionally the backbone of industrial organisation, providing for stability and, to some extent, co-ordination of industrial development. The regulator has always been aware of their central position in the German political economy, but the internationalisation of finance and an increasing tendency of German big players to specialise and become more globally oriented challenges incumbent relationships between industry, banks, labour and politics.[7] Ensuring systemic stability for the national banking sector in times of increasing risks and insecurities while holding 'regulatory costs' for the business at a moderate level to keep them within the country, that is the balance to be striven for by the regulator in both national practice and international negotiation.

Notes

1 See, for instance, *Allgemeiner Teil (AT)* and *Besonderer Teil (BT)* of the *Begründungen* of the Banking Act and its amendments BT-Drs. 7/3657; p. 10; 7/4631; 10/1441 and 3/1114, here pp. 19-20 and especially AT-Abs. II, V, VIII as well as the so-called *Ruhland-Bericht*, Bericht des Wirtschaftsausschusses, BT-Drs. 3/2563, I. 3; III. 1. d; and appendix, p. 2.
2 *Financial Times Deutschland* of 14 March 2000.
3 *Handelsblatt* of 13 April 2000.
4 Two further institutions should be mentioned (Burghof/Rudolfph 1996: 193). First, there is a so-called 'Contact Group', established in 1972 as a very informal forum for national regulators. It is not a formal organ of the EU. Second, the 'Banking Supervisory Subcommittee' was created in 1992 to deal with regulatory issues related to the European Monetary Union.
5 *Verlautbarung* of 8 August 1995, available at http://www.bakred.de
6 As Bähre and Schneider (1986: 50-52) report the history of the *Zins- und Wettbewerbsabkommen* dates back until 1932. Initially created as a cartel of the banks, it was declared a public law (*Allgemeinverfügung*) in 1939 and essentially survived until 1967.

Part III

Conclusion

7

The new regulatory state in perspective

The application of the theory of the regulatory state as an analytical tool to examine developments in statal–societal relations in Germany has offered some surprises to those who believe in a one-dimensional evolutionary process. In fact, and this might be the most important message of this study, the 'regulatory state' in Germany is much less homogeneous than the concept suggests. And even though this work has been confined to only three distinctively different sectors, there is not a single feature which clearly dominates recent developments in all of them. However, as this chapter will show, there are ubiquitous characteristics of the regulatory state in Germany which lie either beyond recent changes or display varying degrees of significance in different sectors.

Before I summarise my findings, I would like to discuss briefly my evaluation of the methodological approach. This work started with three heuristic goals. First, it was intended to be a substantial contribution to *theory* in political science. The frequently used, yet hardly systematised, model of the regulatory state was therefore dismantled and re-assembled so as to make it a usable *analytical* approach to the study of modern statehood and its change both in national and in comparative perspective. Introducing an alternative to the setting of a few testable hypotheses, I have proposed *topoi* as a conceptual tool to bring empirical evidence regarding causal or co-relational relationships under a limited number of headings. I still believe that it is too early to build powerful hypotheses for the German case. It will be left to future research to formulate and test strong hypotheses, thereby contextualising the German case within the group of advanced industrial societies.

Second, this work aimed to present a thorough and well-studied picture of developments in selected sectors in Germany. Emphasising the significance of both the historical foundations as well as the broader constitutional-legal context, I have preferred a wider perspective on the regulatory state instead of only focusing on most recent developments. The latter cannot be understood without reference to which historical and legal background they are based on. This should enable the reader to both acquire a thorough understanding of the regulatory regimes governing telecommunication, broadcasting and banking in Germany and particularly to consider the most important problems involved. Quite often, political science contributions to the study of German political economy, and these sectors in particular, have failed to recognise these open questions and challenges. In that sense, this work is also meant as a substantial contribution to the field of *political economy* within political science.

Third, as well as theoretical considerations and sector-specific revelations, this study presented a comprehensive picture of modern statehood in Germany. The notion of the 'regulatory state' is seen as a useful conceptual tool both to describe and to analyse a very important side of modern states, that is their relations with society and economy. There are, of course, other 'sides', whose importance for the study of statehood I do not deny. However, the 'regulatory' aspect of statehood seems to me particularly interesting, because it virtually suggests itself for comparative purposes: all states in advanced industrial societies have to constantly re-define their role in dealing with societal and economic players. The 'market system', to use Ogus' term once again, is highly dynamic and literally urges the 'collective system' to re-consider its position regarding the former. However, this is not to say that statal change is a simple function depending on society. Rather, changes of the latter represent the context, if not a necessary pre-condition, for statal change, but it is always left to state organs – politics and administration – to assess societal developments and to draw conclusions for their own work. I believe in both multi-causality and multiple causalities. Therefore, only case work can deliver the sort of knowledge needed to generalise and to reconstruct the present state of the German 'regulatory state'. So, finally, I claim this work also contributes to the study of *German government* as a sub-discipline of political science.

Legitimacy regulatory goals compared

The regulatory goals in the sectors studied have never been identical. Moreover, there is no evidence suggesting a clear trend towards, say, *efficiency*, in all three branches. Shifts in the relative weight of regulatory goals have occurred, but they have involved different ones. Figure 7.1 illustrates where we stand today.

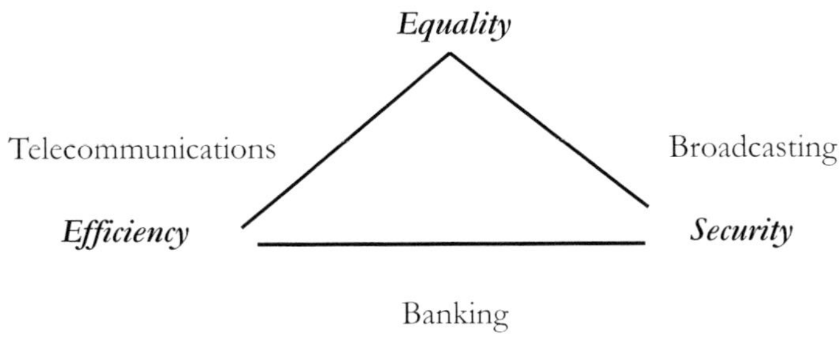

Though the above visualises the findings rather crudely, it points to important differences between the sectors. Broadcasting has seen almost no change, and *efficiency* was and is not a primary matter for regulators in either the private and the public broadcasting systems. Of course, the economic impact of broadcasting as an industry is undeniable. But when looking at the regulatory process in general, and decision-making of the media agencies in the *Länder* in particular, the fostering of 'competition' in an economic sense or the curing of an (economic) market failure does not represent a supreme rationale. Nevertheless, both *Länder* and the media agencies have realised the significance of private broadcasting as an economic sector and it would be unrealistic to assume the regulators' behaviour being uninfluenced by it. Yet 'industrial policy' concerns do not qualify as *efficiency* as such. In fact, the emphasis on *security*, understood as a form of 'social protectionism' of certain moral or societal concerns, stands in opposition to economic goals, and only the future will show whether and in what direction today's balance will shift. Revolutionary developments seem unlikely, as the Federal Constitutional Court has effectively established itself as the 'sovereign' of broadcasting regulation, sanctioning, positively or negatively, all fundamental features of both public and private broadcasting in Germany. In a sense the broadcasting regime is essentially 'judicially' driven, oriented towards mostly 'social' concerns.

Telecommunications has been subject to a more substantial form of change, effectively replacing industrial *protectionism* (of national suppliers) by a prototypical concern about market *efficiency*. The regulator applies not only a range of cures to quite specifically diagnosed market failures, it also aims to pro-actively create a market order, designed to work eventually without regulatory supervision. In a sense, RegTP both substitutes for functions otherwise provided by the market and lays the foundation for a future working market regime, which will render obsolete the 'substitutive' function of the regulator. Yet the telecommunication regime established in the late 1990s has not abandoned social concerns. Not only are suitable instruments provided by the law, but there is also a considerable political pressure on the regulator to keep the issue of *equality* in mind. Nevertheless, the reforms of telecommunication regulation, particularly after *Postreform I*, were essentially 'economically' driven, directed towards a more 'market-oriented' regime.

Interestingly enough, *efficiency* has always been a crucial category for the regulation of banking. However, it has a different meaning here: the 'market failure' problem in finance is not the same as in utilities, where the characteristic product (or service) of the sector inhibits development of a competitive market. Rather, 'systemic stability' is the problem in finance as the whole sector might be in danger if only one player in the market fails. While securing systemic functioning lay at the very beginning of banking regulation, the concern about national competitiveness, hence industrial *protectionism* (as *the* most important form of *security*), has now become more important in the past decade or two and rivals *efficiency*. In order to balance both goals, i.e. systemic stability and the securing of national competitiveness in a global financial market, reforms of banking regulation were largely 'technically' driven, oriented towards greater individualisation of regulation by taking into account the needs of the regulated.

Which causes are responsible for either regime change or regime robustness as far as the *Legitimacy* dimension is concerned? While the introduction of private broadcasting in Germany did not represent a significant shift of regulatory goals, it was brought about by, among other factors, certain party-political ambitions, hence *ideology*. Once technological progress allowed for a 'window of opportunity' to create new forms of broadcasting by introducing an additional, private broadcasting sector, politics used it, but could not provide the new sector with a fundamentally new 'regulatory ideology'. I do not argue that this was ever intended. However, I conclude from my research that even where political ideology becomes effective to massively change institutional structures, this does not necessarily lead to a different set of regulatory goals. Rather, *ideology* must be considered as a category fully independent from seemingly corresponding regulatory goals; *ideology* is certainly *not* a necessary condition to change regulatory goals (as the case of banking illustrates, where it has not played any role), and only generates a corresponding effect on the set of regulatory goals, where and when both institutional pre-conditions and external developments allow for it (as the case of telecommunication reform suggests, where *ideology* was indeed one factor supporting change).

Quite different to broadcasting is the case for telecommunications and banking. There was a shift involving *efficiency* in telecommunications and *security* in banking, entering as new primary regulatory goals. What seems interesting here is that while a multitude of causes accounts for this shift, the *globalisation* of the respective markets for telecommunications and finance has had a decisive impact in both cases. On the one hand, new communication technologies have produced new telecommunication applications and rendered the borders of monopolistic national telecommunication organisations more porous. It seems perfectly reasonable that the federal government answered to these developments by pro-actively establishing a market-oriented regime, which allows society (and the economy) to benefit from 'ordered competition'. On the other hand, the internationalisation of financial markets has similarly shaken up the formerly stable national arrangement of three banking sectors, by providing both new business opportunities and risks, particularly for the big players. With the increasing need to find common rules on the international level, there came about greater national 'protectionism', i.e. concern about the possibly negative consequences of internationally negotiated rules for both national banks and industries. What is worth noticing here is that in both sectors a similar, external development (*globalisation*) has provoked dissimilar consequences for the sectoral regimes. One might wonder whether and to what extent a 'protectionist' strategy for the reform of the telecommunication sector, e.g. by introducing a form of 'single-buyer' model, would have been a viable alternative to the incumbent regime. Obviously, changes in external factors cannot sufficiently account for sectoral development, but must be seen in perspective.

Finally, I shall again emphasise the astonishingly high degree of continuity of the *legitimacy* dimension in all three sectors. While my evaluation of certain developments regarding regulatory goals might be debatable, it is obvious from the findings of this work that there has not been any complete overhaul. Therefore, if we accept the idea that there is a 'new regulatory state' in Germany, it seems safe to conclude that this new state is about new institutions and techniques rather than goals, even though the latter display certain shifts as well.

Agency regulatory institutions compared

The changes in regulatory institutions have been very visible to the public. New agencies have been added (e.g. broadcasting) or have even replaced former institutions (e.g. telecommunications). It is quite easy to overlook the fact that in many other fields there is again continuity. Banking is only one example which in this study stands for a number of 'traditional' cases, whose basic designs date back even earlier than the Second World War.

The emergence of the Federal Financial Services Authority in 2002 stands in no conflict with the continuity hypothesis, as BAFin continues the former BAKred's work on substantially the same organisational basis. I argue that

Table 7.1 Regulatory institutions compared

	Telecommunication	Private broadcasting	Banking
Main regulator	RegTP	Media Agencies of the Länder (LMAs)	BAKred (BAFin since 2002)
Location	Centralised (federal level)	Decentralised (Länder level), but increasing co-operation	Mixed (federal and particularly international levels)
Autonomy	Independence by design & legacy	Independence by imitation & judicial support	Independence by expertise & technicality
Institutional 'rival' and partner for co-operation	BKartA	(KEK)	*Bundesbank*

beyond differences, whose significance shall be evaluated presently, there are characteristic features common to all of them.

In Table 7.1, *public broadcasting* has been omitted as its inclusion in such a comparison would probably lead to misunderstanding. Public broadcasting regulation represents a form of internalised, societally dominated self-regulation, located on the *Länder* level but subject only in part to state supervision and powerfully protected against formal state intrusion by the judiciary. In a sense, public broadcasting challenges the perspective of this work as its regulatory design touches the borders between 'regulation' and 'corporate governance'. However, it is included because I believe it provides an important insight into one variation of 'regulation', which is relevant also to the understanding of private broadcasting. I shall refer to the public system on several occasions in the following pages, but will turn now to a summarising evaluation of the table.

What is obvious from a comparative perspective is one feature common to all sectors: relative institutional *independence* of the regulator(s). In none of these sectors is the government itself the single most important regulator, even though it is, with differing degrees, involved in the regulatory process. Furthermore, institutional independence of the regulators has been generated by a variety of forces, the relevant set being different in each sector.

With the final step of *Postreform III*, RegTP was established as a separate regulatory agency. Its autonomy stems from two sources in particular, i.e. the *design* of its internal organisation (with court-like 'decision-taking chambers') and the *legacy* of its institutional roots in a ministry. Contrary to the case of telecommunications, the BAKred's institutional independence may be related to two other sources, or factors, merely generated by the regulatory subject matter as such. First, the issues the regulator is concerned with in practice have reached an enormous level of *technicality*, which seem even less suitable for political deliberation than what RegTP deals with. After all, decisions of the latter, such as licensing, have an immediate effect on the market as they merely 'create' or at least substantially shape 'markets' where there had not been any before. The banking market, on the other hand, is not equally affected by new players. Regulatory work here has become more removed from spectacular action, frequently praised or condemned in the press, as is the case with RegTP. Second, the high degree of technicality in banking regulation necessitates regulators to acquire a similarly sophisticated *expertise*. Neither politics nor its administrative backbone in the ministries are able to catch up.

What was true for BAKred holds for its successor BAFin. Owing to its particular legal form, with a supervisory board above the president, as well as a separate budget financed by contributions and fees paid by the regulated, independence has only been further secured.

Finally, the media agencies' autonomy in regulating private broadcasting seems due to two aspects. They have largely borrowed institutional structures from public broadcasting, e.g. integration of societal groups, forming a pluralistic body to decide on the more fundamental regulatory questions. This approach to *imitation* of an organisational safeguard, recognised by the courts as an important feature of the state-free public broadcasting system, illustrates, however, only in part what enormous impact the 'third branch' had in the shaping of both the public and the private broadcasting regimes. It is this *judicial support*, manifested in a range of rulings since the first major decision in 1961, which accounts so much not only for institutional arrangements found in broadcasting, but also for the relative robustness of regulatory goals and, to a lesser extent, the practice of regulatory action by the media agencies.

As opposed to the aspect of 'independence', the assignment of regulatory power to either the federal or the *Länder* level reveals important differences. Leaving aside aspects of increasing European harmonisation, which has affected all sectors to different extents since the late 1970s and particularly since the mid-1980s, the location of regulatory institutions at different levels of government reflects the constitutional doctrine of the Basic Law in the 'separation of powers': what might be surprising to some is not so much the fact that there *is* distribution of competencies, but that there had been such fundamental conflicts over it. Neither in broadcasting nor in the regulation of banking was there unanimous consent in the 1950s about 'what the law is'. The Federal Constitutional Court had to resolve the conflict between federal government and *Länder* governments, deciding in favour of the first in the case of banking and in favour of the second in the case of broadcasting. Telecommunications saw less controversy, although the debate on the *Infrastrukturrat* in the early 1990s illustrates that German *federalism* has been a factor of primary importance up to today regarding institutional arrangements everywhere, even when the constitutional matters seem absolutely clear.

Table 7.1 simplifies the issue by categorising 'location' as 'centralised', 'decentralised' and 'mixed'. While the case of telecommunications is rather obvious, both broadcasting and banking need additional explanation. The banking regime is, of course, primarily a federal matter and it is administered by a federal agency. However, as mentioned in Chapter 6, there are not only *Länder* regimes, governing the savings bank sector, which, at least in part, are 'regulatory' in the sense of the concept as used in this work; but the *Basle Committee* has also acquired outstanding importance, which goes far beyond what international organisations or fora mean in either broadcasting or telecommunications.

The regulation of both public and private broadcasting is, *prima facie*, decentralised. However, in neither the public nor the private broadcasting systems are *Länder* governments or LMAs really free to pursue their own policies. On the one hand, the simple necessity to find uniform solutions for national programmes has motivated, if not forced, media agencies to co-operate. The same holds essentially true for public broadcasting, as the independent ARD corporations had to co-ordinate their efforts to establish the first national TV programme and, later, ARD and ZDF realised that co-operation would generate both political and economic synergies. On the other hand, the highest court stopped some *Länder* governments from engaging in a form of 'separatism'. What has emerged is what I would call *limping federalism*, because first, *Länder* are not fully able to live out their (political) 'diversity' regarding a range of issues and, second, regional differences prevail under the permanent *proviso* of the judiciary.

Assuming 'sovereignty' of any domestic regulatory institution in the age of 'Europeanisation' is, of course, anachronistic and out of place. Furthermore, this idea never fitted in anyhow with some of the German legalistic-administrative traditions, such as the high codification of executive work. However, even beyond European and legalistic restrictions, we find that regulators are accompanied by fellow institutions in charge of near-regulatory matters. In the case of banking, it is the *Bundesbank*, which substituted for the missing organisational infrastructure of the BAKred, and has now increasingly developed into an institutional rival to the banking regulator, as monetary policy-making has been taken out of its hands. In the case of telecommunications, it was the BKartA, largely deprived of power, now transferred to the EU Commission due to the 'Europeanisation' of cartel law, which tried unsuccessfully to have RegTP tasks incorporated. However, due to the characteristics of the regulatory problems involved in telecommunications, co-operation between RegTP and BKartA is unavoidable today and for the near future. Finally, while there is no federal 'rival' for the media agencies, the *Länder* governments have exhibited proof of their ability to successfully exercise their remaining regulatory discretion by establishing an expert commission, the KEK, to deal with the concentration problem in the media sector. Thereby, the media agencies lost an important regulatory task, formerly tackled in co-operative efforts. However, the difficulties preceeding the creation of KEK illustrate the main problem of a decentralised organisation of regulatory institutions, which is the constant search and struggle for the *unité de doctrine* needed in a country, where the 'rule of law' not only has a quite distinct meaning, but also enjoys a degree of supremacy unmatched in most other advanced industrial societies.

Interestingly, the KEF, a semi-political body set up in the 1970s to recommend on financial issues of public broadcasting, had been transformed into an expert commission through a decision made by the Federal Constitutional Court. Similarly to KEK, the KEF also stands for an attempt to assign important regulatory functions to experts, recruited from society and independent from both politics, administration and (though partly unsuccessfully in the case of KEK) the regulated. Beyond the goal of the *unité de doctrine*, 'expert regulation' tackles the problem of *politicisation* in order to render its decision-making process 'court-proof'. As the latter provides high legitimacy, it is hardly surprising that, for instance, KEF recommendations on broadcasting fees are usually followed closely by *Länder* governments.

The causes which account for institutional change and robustness in the three sectors studied here are complex. While the sector-specific melange of *globalisation*, *technological progress* and increasing *European integration* (mostly by generating or harmonising common standards, rules and norms) has provided the context for regulatory reform in each of the sectors studied (Chapters 4, 5 and 6 describe their relative significance in detail), there are also identifiable factors accounting more precisely for institutional developments. First, in telecommunications, the establishment of RegTP seems inexplicable without reference to different forms of policy learning. Not only has it obviously been inspired by the sector-specific institutional arrangements implemented in other countries, but the regime's sponsors have also borrowed from other indigenous models, such as the BKartA. Nevertheless, the survival of an organ where *Länder* interests are represented illustrates the significance of German *federalism*.

Second, one could assume that the modelling of media agencies in the private broadcasting sector has similarly been a case of 'policy learning'. However, this variation of institutional imitation was not due to any 'learning', but to quite simple judicial 'mandating'. In fact, there was not much discretion left. Societal representation in a pluralistic body serves in both cases the 'diversity' doctrine of the Federal Constitutional Court; while only in the case of public broadcasting is it formally 'endogenous' and in the case of private broadcasting is it formally 'exogenous', incorporated in the media agencies. However, beyond the judicial aspect, pluralistic, societal representation in broadcasting also meets a mere political function; that is, it generates legitimisation of decisions deemed very important to society and, of course, the sector, for example programme schemes, licences or licence revocation.

Third, in the banking sector, there has not been any significant institutional change of the BAKreduntil 2002. In a sense, BAKred has proved successful (including the sharing of powers with the *Bundesbank*). However, one might question whether this was due to institutional design or to the regulatory culture of the sector, which provided sufficient legitimacy *eo ipso*, so that either 'acceptance-generating' institutions (such as media councils) or 'quasi-judicial' bodies (such as decision-taking chambers – rendering the decision-making process 'court-proof') have been unnecessary. With the creation of BAFin, however, a new era in fanace regulation has begun.

The above leads to an important aspect of regime reform, i.e. the issue of provision of 'legitimisation by institution(s)'. This is not only a crucial element of any institutional arrangement set in place to exercise regulatory activities, but also a feature common to the reform process itself. There had been *expert commissions*, partly quasi-corporatist and partly not, established in the course of reforming the sectors at different stages and with varying impact on the reform outcome: the Witte Kommission, which presented its recommendations for the reform of the telecommunication sector in 1987; the *KtK*, proposing the cable pilot projects as a prerequisite for private broadcasting in the late 1970s; and the *Wettbewerbsenquête* as well as the *Bankenstrukturkommission* of the late 1960s and 1970s, whose recommendations of a self-administered deposit protection scheme or the consolidation of accounting data respectively became similarly part of reform legislation. As outlined in the chapters of Part II, there had been considerable debate as to how much impact each of these expert bodies effectively had. Viewed in retrospect, I tend to believe that their function was to legitimise rather than to advise. Admittedly, this is a little speculative and I would like to emphasise that there is no conclusive proof. However, there are two reasons in particular which make me engage in such speculation. First, historical analysis shows that there had been 'time inconsistencies' both of these expert recommendations (e.g. reform of DBP) and political or ministerial 're-actions' in the case of telecommunications as well as of realising such proposals (e.g. the cable pilot project) and subsequent 'evaluation' (i.e. the passage of media acts before assessment of the pilot projects) in the case of broadcasting. Second, the results of expert commissions' deliberations have been used quite selectively. Rather than viewing their reports as a comprehensive conception for reform, politics and/or ministerial bureaucracies have related to single elements, as illustrated by the reforms in the banking sector. At best, the commissions' work has been used as a 'pool' of reform ideas.

Compliance regulatory instruments and modes compared

The regulatory instruments in all three sectors, as provided by the respective laws, are not only directed at similar regulatory problems, such as 'market entry', 'market behaviour' or 'market exit', but also include the full range of modes, from 'command and control' measures, governed by criminal law, to 'moral suasion', backed primarily by institutional reputation or a mutually trustful relationship. As described in detail in Part II, the application of strong or weak, formal or informal modes of regulation vary considerably not only cross-sectorally, but also within each sector. A complete listing of all details would obscure the implications rather than illuminate them at this point. Therefore, Table 7.2 summarises essential features according to four significant aspects.

Table 7.2 Regulatory instruments and modes compared

	Telecommunications	**Private broadcasting**	**Banking**
Approach	Asymmetrical	Symmetrical	From symmetrical to asymmetrical
Pro-active regulation	Creation of competitive market	Creation of 'diversity' in broadcasting	Creation of level playing field internationally
Re-active regulation	Abuse of or non-compliance with market behaviour regulation	Most other issues; often 'soft' and informal	Most other issues; often 'soft', but formal
Court involvement in regulatory process	Important	Decisive	Modest (for banks); Important (for financial service institutions)

Again, I have not included the regulation of public broadcasting as the above categories would probably misdescribe the reality of public broadcasting regulation. The following text will, however, relate to public broadcasting and shed light on it.

The regulatory approaches are quite different in substance, but they have a potential to change. Telecommunication regulation is designed asymmetrically, that is the former monopolist is subject to more restrictive regulatory interference than its competitors. This seems inevitable, considering the goal of creating a working market regime where there had been none before. Contrary to telecommunications, the regulation of private broadcasting is not confronted with a dominant incumbent player *governed* by this regime. Rather, the incumbents are subject to another regulatory regime (that is the essence of the *dual broadcasting order*) and in fact, they form a fully separate group of 'regulated', intersecting with private broadcasters only where new frequencies are to be assigned. Of course, there is a problem of 'market dominance' in private broadcasting, too, and there is increasing awareness. But it poses a different set of problems than an incumbent network operator in telecommunications, whose infrastructure is effectively needed by all players in the market.

Banking regulation was established with a symmetrical approach in the first place; the idea was that any bank failure might cause systemic failure and therefore discrimination between differently regulated types of bank seemed illogical. Apart from that, the above rationale for asymmetrical regulation in telecommunication, i.e. access to a decisive device needed for market entry, was irrelevant in finance. However, present developments suggest a certain shift from the symmetrical, quantitative and relatively rigid approach implemented in the regime and consequently pursued by the BAKred in the past towards an asymmetrical one. It does not make sense to hold smaller banks, operating only domestically, subject to the same sophisticated rules, designed to cope with the enormous and complex risks of big players operating in the global market. While this is not the same notion of 'asymmetry' as in telecommunications, it is related to a similar rationale: in order to safeguard the competitiveness of different banks in their markets, different instruments, with a varying degree of 'severity', are needed.

Interestingly, each sectoral regime contains regulatory elements of both 'pro-activism' and 're-activism'. This is quite obvious in the telecommunication sector. On the one hand, RegTP has to enable competitors to enter the market, thereby virtually creating it. On the other hand, the regulator monitors market developments, e.g. prices, and intervenes if market behaviour endangers the sustainability of the market (e.g. by unfair practices, such as price dumping). As opposed to both other sectors, regulation of the liberalised telecommunication sector is fairly recent and there has not been sufficient time to allow for a distinct 'culture' of relations between regulator and the regulated. Thus, it seems hardly surprising that the regulated are very much inclined to go to court if the regulator's decision seems unfavourable to them. A lawsuit on average every other day speaks for itself. Decision-making by RegTP is therefore highly formalised and 'court-proof' to meet what is needed in the post-administrative phase in the courthouse.

Similar to telecommunications, it was the media agencies' primary task to establish and ensure a certain degree of 'diversity' within the private broadcasting sector by means of both licensing and providing framework requirements for the programme schemes. As seen in Chapter 5, the regulators had set up formal licensing procedures to render their decision-making transparent to both applicants and the public. While the creation and preservation of 'diversity' is a permanent challenge to be dealt with by the regulators, it has lost some of its significance for their daily practice. Media agencies now have to focus on issues of actual 'market behaviour', identifying offences with protection clauses, restrictions on commercials and the like. Their work has become, in many areas, somewhat re-active, but nevertheless, media agencies tend to rely on 'informal' regulatory interference rather than formal orders (even though they could). Informality is here connected to low severity, i.e. soft regulation, as regulators strive to settle disagreements in informal talks with members of the executive body. So the vast majority of problems never reach the quasi-public level of the media council.

For the past decade or so, the banking regulator has begun to retreat from the former rigid approach and incorporated more flexible instruments to tackle regulatory problems brought about by the internationalisation of finance. At least as far as the big German players in the global market are concerned, BAKred, and is inclined to take care that the supervisory rules, mostly negotiated in Basle, do not structurally hamper the competitiveness of German banks. For a long time, this was more 're-active', but the European countries in the Committee have realised that they must come up with their own solutions. In a sense, the global financial market, or better, its co-ordinated international regulation, is still *in statu nascendi* and thus features a certain similarity to the emergence of a (yet primarily domestic) telecommunication market in Germany. Although such 'pro-activism' demanded from the regulator seems to represent a novelty in the history of German banking regulation, it is, in fact, not so. Right after its establishment in 1961, BAKred began to encourage and support mergers of smaller banks to make them less vulnerable to market risks. Nevertheless, BAKred activities were usually oriented towards identifying 'black sheep', i.e. revealing violations of the law and re-acting accordingly. The regulator was, by virtue of its sheer size, unable to pursue a 'case-by-case' approach on a larger scale. Rather, it 'informed' the regulated – mostly via their associations – about its view on certain issues in (formal) circulatory letters. As the regulated have always been willing to comply, not in the least in order to achieve regulatory 'predictability', in the vast number of cases more 'severe' measures, backed by threats, were not necessary. Over the years, a regulatory culture of mutual trust and predictability had emerged and it helped to prevent massive reliance on judicial review. It was only with the inclusion of another sort of 'regulated', the financial service institutions, that actions by BAKred became more formalised, connected with 'hard' obligations on the regulated, and, of course, increasingly subject to judicial review.

What I found common to all three regulatory regimes is a certain practice of regulators to bind themselves to rules, even where the law grants them more discretion. In telecommunications, the regulator set up complex schemes of a decentralised decision-making process governing licensing in order to be able to show proof of each stage. Obviously, accountability to the judiciary (not necessarily to the public!) is valued extremely highly – and the fact that the regulated have no hesitation to go to court proves them right. Furthermore, RegTP has most recently turned to 'auctioning', which in itself is a procedure where no discretion is left to the regulator. In banking, the BAKred has traditionally sent circular letters and even though they qualify as 'soft regulation' (because they present an official opinion rather than a public command) they are a case in point. And finally, media agencies have, since the beginning of private broadcasting in Germany, co-operated not in the least to find common rules applicable to each one of them: only by way of co-ordinating the basic principles upon which their case-specific decisions, e.g. licensing or sanctioning a violation against a protection clause, are based, were they able to create equal conditions in the whole country and render their decision-making more transparent. Similarly, each agency has formalised the licensing procedures, as mentioned above. Maybe, formalisation of decision-making is, if not a necessity, a likely corollary of 'pro-activist' regulation as the cases of telecommunications and broadcasting suggest. There would, at least, be a good reason for regulators to do so: assuming that 'pro-activist' regulation is of a different quality than 're-active', in a sense 'disturbing' the *status quo* and hence the relative position of the (incumbent) regulated, the latter are often more inclined to seek assistance from outside, i.e. the judiciary. While this view ignores prima facie the 'regulatory culture' of the respective sector, it might point to a more general tendency of regulatory behaviour by both regulators and the regulated.

Be that as it may, the self-binding to rules by German administration in general, and regulators in particular, has often been said to exemplify a certain *legalistic culture*. While the term is, as such, a mere synonym for this very observation, it might actually obscure in many cases what stands behind it. Setting up rules, even where the law provides for discretion, and binding oneself to them increases predictability for the regulated. They can count on a certain practice. Thereby, such self-restriction of regulators supports the emergence of mutual trust and reliability. This is not only advantageous for the regulated, but also for the regulator: if disagreement cannot be settled and the case goes to court, the regulator has a better chance to win the case, as it complies with the requirements usually applied by judges. In a sense, a substantial part of German 'legalism' is due to

German *judicialism*.

If we turn to the forces accounting for a change in the regime as far as the *Compliance* dimension is concerned, we find quite different scenarios in the sectors. The choice of regulatory instruments and modes in broadcasting, both in the law books and in practice, has been largely 'court-driven'. It was the Federal Constitutional Court who not only set up the basic doctrines, hence *ideology*, governing both public and private broadcasting, but also to, explicitly or implicitly, determine the way its ideology was given 'regulatory life'. For one thing, it is inevitable that media agencies should fear that applicants turned down in the licensing procedures may go to court. Therefore, these procedures had to be designed 'court-proof'. Moreover, when the highest court began to emphasise the individual right to broadcast this was understood as a 'recommendation' not to restrict the editorial freedom of private broadcasters more than absolutely necessary. Thus, media agencies have since been reluctant to apply hard sanctions.

While some of the above also holds for the telecommunication regime, there are qualitative differences. First of all, the telecommunication regime has borrowed both regulatory procedures (e.g. auctioning or 'price capping') and regulatory doctrines (e.g. the 'essential facilities' doctrine) from Anglo-American origins. In that sense, policy learning represents an important characteristic in the emergence of the regulatory instruments of the incumbent regime. However, such innovations, mostly novel, if not foreign to German administration, had to be reconciled with the German understanding of the 'rule of law'. Again, it is the significance of *judicialism* which accounts for the legal implementation and, of course, adaptation, of these regulatory 'imports'. Whereas European law has influenced regulatory techniques in the broadcasting sector only in part (e.g. protection clauses and regulation of commercials in particular) it had a much more concrete impact on the shape of regulatory instruments in the telecommunication regime; a large number of Directives and other legal sources have effectively narrowed down their scope, leaving much less discretion with the law-makers in telecommunication. In broadcasting, of course, their scope of action had already been restricted by the judiciary.

Finally, the causes for change in regulatory techniques of the banking regime have shifted in the late 1970s and early 1980s. Until that time, *crises* had been the major stimulus of reform. A major banking crisis in the early 1930s was a decisive influence at the very beginning of the regime as a whole, including the instruments provided by the law. Subsequent reforms, such as in 1976 and even in 1984 can be linked to preceeding problems in the market. Consequently, the reforms included new instruments and rules tackling exactly the causes of these crises. However, after the EC Commission regained interest in regulating banking in the early 1980s, reforms of the banking regime were transformed into mere reflexes of EU law developments. Yet, the latter are themselves not the outcome of a sovereign process of law-making. Rather, the Basle process has largely influenced, if not dominated the implementation of new rules at the European level and, subsequently, in municipal law.

A New State?

The new regulatory state in Germany exists in a range of sector-specific variations, none of which is equal to the other. Differences may partly be attributed to the length of their respective incumbency. However, even then, we find no 'evolutionary law' governing their change over time. 'Regulation' has always been available as a form of governance, but it was found useful in different sectors at different points in time. Furthermore, its very appearance, visible in goals, institutions and instruments, was similarly subject to change. Therefore, whilst there is no 'new state', there have been enormous changes in statehood.

Nevertheless, can we gain a more comprehensive picture of the present state of the German statehood, if we generalise from the details? Yes, I believe, we can. First, in all three sectors studied, private players have gained additional room for manoeuvre if compared with the late 1970s. There is now a 'market system' in each of the sectors. Second, this general trend towards liberalisation does not, however, by any means imply reduction or abolition of rules and norms governing the sectors. There is no general or sectoral 'race to the bottom', not even where this hypothesis might make most sense. But 'new regulation' is often more flexible and responsive than 'old regulation', which, of course, increases its acceptance by the regulated.

Third, institutional independence of the regulators in all three sectors is accompanied by a tendency on the part of regulators to create 'self-binding rules'. Even where innovative regulatory techniques have been introduced, German regulators hesitate to apply them with discretion. Passing relatively precise administrative guidelines governing the daily work of regulators seems '*legalistic*' in the first place, but I suspect it to be a mere outcome of German '*judicialism*'. However, it is interesting to note that administrative preference for 'self-binding' appears to exist quite independently from the 'regulatory culture' of the respective sector. Obviously, where the regulator has not yet built up a reputation as a reliable partner, such 'self-binding' strategies help to stand the test of judicial review; and where mutual trust has grown as a result of long-term co-operation between the regulator and the regulated, these rules reinforce the regulator's reliability by making its action predictable.

Fourth, *globalisation*, *European integration* and *technical progress* account, of course for a great deal of change in all three sectors. In a sense, German statehood might be said to have further lost its 'sovereignty' as it increasingly becomes dependent on exogenous developments, whose impact the state cannot control. However, neither of the above factors is able to sufficiently account for any sectoral regime, far less for the 'state of the state' as a whole. This comes as a surprise only to those who have ignored the power of German federalism. The constitutional distribution of legislative competencies and of public property as well as the different interests of both the federal government and the *Länder* has profoundly shaped the basis, the process and the outcome of regulatory reforms, thereby lending the discussion of the 'new regulatory state' another, important dimension.

Finally, I would add that regulatory developments range from spectacular innovations to silent (r)evolutions. As stated before, there has been much change, but it does not follow a single-dimensional course. Nevertheless, the state in its various organs and at its various levels has proved capable of 'change', partly adapting itself to the unavoidable and partly deliberately steering the process. By any means, 'German statehood' is not a lethargic and gigantic remnant of the past, but a body, which has shown evidence of being 'governable'. In spite of some sectoral differences regarding its 'governability', there is hope that the state has preserved its ability to achieve reforms.

Bibliography

Introduction

Abbott, Andrew (1983) 'Sequences of Social Events', *Historical Methods* 16, pp. 129–147.

Abelshauser, Werner (1991) 'Die ordnungspolitische Bedeutung der Weltwirtschaftskrise in Deutschland: Ein Beitrag zur Geschichte der Sozialen Marktwirtschaft', in Petzina, D. (ed) *Ordnungspolitische Weichenstellungen nach dem Zweiten Weltkrieg*. Berlin: Duncker & Humblot.

Ayres, Ian & Braithwaite, John (1995) *Responsive Regulation. Transcending the Deregulation Debate*. New York: Oxford University Press.

Bain, Joe S. (1968) *Industrial Organization*. New York: Wiley.

Becker, Howard S. (1992) 'Cases, Causes, Conjunctures, Stories, and Imagery', in Ragin, Charles C. & Becker, Howard S. (eds) *What is a Case? Exploring the Foundations of Social Inquiry*. Cambridge: Cambridge University Press, pp. 205–216.

Benz, Angelika & König, Klaus (1997) 'Privatisierung und staatliche Regulierung – eine Zwischenbilanz', in König, Klaus & Benz, Angelika (eds) *Privatisierung und staatliche Regulierung. Bahn, Post und Telekommunikation, Rundfunk*. Baden-Baden: Nomos, pp. 606–650.

Brown, Harold I. (1987) *Observation and Objectivity*. New York: Oxford University Press.

Buchanan, James M., Tollison, Robert D. & Tullock, Gordon (eds) (1980) *Toward a Theory of the Rent-Seeking Society*. College Station: Texas A&M Press.

Bulmer, Simon (1992) 'Completing the European Community's Internal Market: The Regulatory Implications for the Federal Republic of Germany', Dyson, Kenneth (ed) *The Politics of German Regulation*. Aldershot: Dartmouth, pp. 53–78.

Caporaso, James A. & Levine, David P. (1992) *Theories of Political Economy*. Cambridge: Cambridge UP.

Clark, John Maurice (1940) 'Toward a Concept of Workable Competition', *American Economic Review* 30, pp. 241–256.

Cook, Thomas D. & Campbell, Donald T. (1979) *Quasi-Experimentation. Design and Analysis Issues for Field Settings*. Boston: Houghton Mifflin.

Currie, David P. (1994) *The Constitution of the Federal Republic of Germany*. Chicago: University of Chicago Press.

DeMuth, Christopher C. (1983) 'What is Regulation?', Zeckhauser, Richard, J. & Leebaert, Derek (eds) *What Role for Government? Lessons from Policy Research*. Durham: Duke University Press, pp. 262–279.

Derthick, M. & Quirk, P.J. (1985) *The Politics of Deregulation*. Washington, D.C.: Brookings Institution.

Dyson, Kenneth (ed) (1992) *The Politics of German Regulation*. Aldershot: Dartmouth.

Dyson, Kenneth (1992a) 'Regulatory Culture and Regulatory Change: some Conclusions', Dyson, Kenneth (ed) *The Politics of German Regulation*. Aldershot: Dartmouth, pp. 257–271.

Edwards, Corwin D. (1956) *Big Business and the Policy of Competition.* Cleveland: Press of Western Reserve University.

Eisner, Marc A. (1992) *Regulatory Politics in Transition.* Baltimore: The Johns Hopkins University Press.

Eucken, Walter (1952) *Grundsätze der Wirtschaftspolitik.* Tübingen: Mohr &Siebeck..

Ferguson, Christopher E. (1964) *A Macroeconomic Theory of Workable Competition.* Durham, N.C.: Duke University Press.

Field, Alexander James (1984) 'Microeconomics, Norms, and Rationality', *Economic Development and Cultural Change* 32, no. 4, pp. 683–712.

Francis, John G. (1993) *The Politics of Regulation. A Comparative Perspective.* Oxford: Blackwell 1993.

Gellner, Ernest (1985) *Relativism and the Social Sciences.* Cambridge: Cambridge University Press.

von Gierke, Otto (1868) *Das deutsche Genossenschaftsrecht.* Volume 1. Berlin: Weidmann.

Gourevitch, Peter (1986) *Politics in Hard Times: Comparative Responses to International Economic Crises.* Ithaca: Cornell University Press.

Grimm, Dieter in cooperation with Evelyn Hagenah (ed) (1996) *Staatsaufgaben.* Frankfurt a.M.: Suhrkamp.

Handler, Milton (1990) 'Regulation versus Competition', Handler, Milton: *Antitrust in Transition.* Volume 1. Ardsley-on-Hudson: Transnational Juris, pp. 131–145.

Hall, Peter (1986) *Governing the Economy. The Politics of State Intervention in Britain and France.* Oxford: Oxford University Press.

Harris, Richard A. & Milkis, Sidney, M. (1996) *The Politics of Regulatory Change. A Tale of Two Agencies.* New York: Oxford University Press.

Hart, Jefffrey A. (1992) *Rival Capitalists. International Competitiveness in the United States, Japan, and Western Europe.* Ithaca: Cornell University Press.

Von Hayek, Friedrich A. (1973, 1976, 1979) *Law, Legislation and Liberty.* Volume 1,2 and 3. Chicago: University of Chicago Press.

Héritier, Adrienne, Mingers, Susanne, Knill, Christoph & Becka, Martina (1994) *Die Veränderung von Staatlichkeit in Europa. Ein regulativer Wettbewerb: Deutschland, Großbritannien und Frankreich in der Europäischen Union.* Opladen: Leske und Budrich.

Joskow, Paul L. & Noll, Roger C. (1981) 'Regulation in Theory and Practice: An Overview, Fromm, Gary (ed) *Studies in Public Regulation.* Cambridge, Mass.: MIT Press, pp. 1–65.

Kantzenbach, Erhard (1967) *Die Funktionsfähigkeit des Wettbewerbs.* 2. edition. Göttingen: Vandenhoeck & Ruprecht.

Katzenstein, Peter J. (ed) (1978) *Between Power and Plenty: Foreign Economic Policies of Advanced Industrial States.* Madison: University of Wisconsin Press.

Katzenstein, Peter (1989) 'Stability and Change in the Emerging Third Republic', Katzenstein, Peter (ed) *Industry and Politics in West Germany: Toward the Third Republic.* Ithaca: Cornell University Press, pp. 307–353.

King, Gary, Keohane, Robert O. & Verba, Sidney (1994) *Designing Social Inquiry: Scientific nference in Qualitative Research.* Princeton: Princeton University Press.

Köttgen, Arnold (1927) 'Gewerbegesetzgebung', *Handwörterbuch der Staatswissenschaften.* 4th edition. 4th Volume. Jena: Fischer, pp. 1000–1054.

Krasner, Stephan D. (1983) 'Structural Causes and Regime Consequences: Regimes as Intervening Variables', Krasner, Stephan D. (ed) *International Regimes.* Ithaca: Cornell University Press, pp. 1–21.

Leaman, Jeremy (1994) 'Regulatory Reform and Privatization in Germany', Moran,

Michael & Prosser, Tony (eds) *Privatization and Regulatory Change in Europe*. Buckingham: Open University Press, pp. 14–34.

Machlup, Ferdinand (1952) *The Political Economy of Monopoly*. Baltimore: The Johns Hopkins University Press.

Majone, Giandomenico (1994) 'The Rise of the Regulatory State in Europe', *West European Politics*, 17, no. 3, pp. 77–101.

Majone, Giandomenico (1996a) 'Theories of Regulation', Majone, Giandomenico (ed) *Regulating Europe*. London: Routledge, pp. 28–46.

Majone, Giandomenico (1996b) 'Regulation and Its Modes', Majone, Giandomenico (ed) *Regulating Europe*. London: Routledge, pp. 9–27.

Mitchell, Timothy (1991) 'The Limits of the State: Beyond Statist Approaches and their Critics', *American Political Science Review* 85 (1991), no. 1, pp. 77–96.

Mösbauer, Heinz (1990) *Staatsaufsicht über die Wirtschaft*. Köln: Carl Heymann.

Moran, Michael & Prosser, Tony (1994) 'Introduction: Politics, Privatization and Constitutions', Moran, Michael & Prosser, Tony (eds) *Privatization and Regulatory Change in Europe*. Buckingham: Open University Press, pp. 1–13.

Müller, Jürgen & Vogelsang, Ingo (1979) *Staatliche Regulierung. Regulated Industries in den USA und Gemeinwohlbindung in wettbewerblichen Ausnahmebereichen in der Bundesrepublik Deutschland*. Baden-Baden: Nomos.

Müller, Markus M. (1996) 'Deregulierung und Privatisierung aus ökonomischer Sicht', Sturm, Roland & Wilks, Stephen (eds) *Wettbewerbspolitik und die Ordnung der Elektrizitätswirtschaft in Deutschland ud Großbritannien*. Baden-Baden: Nomos, pp. 11–52.

Müller, Markus M. & Sturm, Roland (1998) 'Ein neuer regulativer Staat in Deutschland? die neuere Theory of the Regulatory State und ihre Anwendbarkeit in der deutschen Staatswissenschaft', *Staatswissenschaften und Staatspraxis* 3, pp. 385–412.

Müller-Armack, Alfred (1976) *Wirtschaftsordnung und Wirtschaftspolitik*. Bern und Stuttgart: Paul Haupt.

Niskanen, William A. (1971) *Bureaucracy and Representative Government*. Chicago: Aldine.

Niskanen, William A. (1994) *Bureaucracy and Public Enterprise*. Aldershot and Brookfield: Edward Elgar.

Noll, Roger C. (1983) 'The Political Foundations of Regulatory Policy', *Zeitschrift für die gesamte Staatswissenschaft* 139 (1983), pp. 377–404.

Noll, Roger C. & Owen, Bruce (1983) *The Political Economy of Deregulation*. Washington, D.C.: Brookings Institute.

O'Connor, James R. (1973) *The Fiscal Crisis of the State*. New York: St. Martin's Press.

Ogus, Anthony (1996) *Regulation. Legal Form and Economic Theory*. Oxford: Clarendon Press.

Owen, Bruce M. & Braeutigam, Ronald (1978) *The Regulation Game*. Cambridge, Mass.: Ballinger Publishing Company.

Parson, Talcott (1937) *The Structure of Social Action*. New York: McGraw-Hill.

Peltzman, Sam (1976) 'Toward a More General Theory of Regulation', *Journal of Law and Economics*, 19 (August), pp. 211–240.

Polanyi, Karl (1944) *The Great Transformation*. New York: Farrar & Rinehart.

Polanyi, Karl (1957) 'Aristotle Discovers the Economy', Polanyi, Karl, Arensberg, Conrad, M. & Pearson, Harry W. (eds) *Trade and Market in the Early Empires. Economies in History and Theory*. Glencoe: Free Press, pp.64–94.

Popper Karl R. (1959) *The Logic of Scientific Discovery*. New York: Basic Books.

Posner, Richard (1973) *Economic Analysis of Law*. Boston: Little, Brown.
Posner, Richard (1974) 'Theories of Economic Regulation', *Bell Journal of Economics and Management Science* (1974), 5, pp. 335–358.
Ragin, Charles C. (1987) *The Comparative Method: Moving Beyond Qualitative and Quantitative Strategies*. Berkeley: University of California Press.
Ragin, Charles C. (1992) '"Casing" and the Process of Social Inquiry', Ragin, Charles C. & Becker, Howard S. (eds) *What is a Case? Exploring the Foundations of Social Inquiry*. Cambridge: Cambridge University Press, pp. 217–226.
Ragin, Charles C. (1992a) 'Introduction: Cases of "What is a case?"', Ragin, Charles C. & Becker, Howard S. (eds) *What is a Case? Exploring the Foundations of Social Inquiry*. Cambridge: Cambridge University Press, pp. 1–17.
Rawls, John (1955) 'Two Concepts of Justice', *Philosophical Review* 64, pp. 3–33.
Rittberger, Volker (1995) 'Research on International Regimes in Germany: The Adaptive Internalization of an American Social Science Conept', Rittberger, Volker (edited with the assistance of Peter Mayer) *Regime Theory and International Relations*. Oxford: Clarendon University Press, pp. 3–22.
Rogerson, William (1982) 'The Social Costs of Monopoly and Regulation: A Game-Theoretic Analysis', *The Bell Journal of Economics* 13 (1982), pp. 391–401.
Rose-Ackerman, Susanne (1992) *Rethinking the Progressive Agenda: The Reform of the American Regulatory State*. New York: The Free Press.
Schliesky, Utz (1997) *Öffentliches Wettbewerbsrecht. Verhaltensrechtliche Determinanten von wirtschaftsbezogenem Staatshandeln*. Berlin: Duncker & Humblot.
Schmidt, Ingo (1996) *Wettbewerbspolitik und Kartellrecht. Eine Einführung*. 5. edition. Stuttgart: Lucius & Lucius.
von Schönberg, Gustav (1896) *Handbuch der politischen Ökonomie*. 2nd Volume. 1st Half-binding. 4th edition. Tübingen: Laupp.
Seidman, H. & Gilmour, R. (1986) *Politics, Position and Power: From the Positive to the Regulatory State*. 4th edition. Oxford University Press.
Stigler, George (1971) 'The Theory of Economic Regulation', *Bell Journal of Economics and Management Science* 2 (Spring), pp. 3–21.
Stober, Rolf (1989) *Handbuch des Wirtschaftsverwaltungs- und Umweltrechts*. Stuttgart.
Stone, Alan (1977) *Economic Regulation and the Public Interest: The Federal Trade Commission in Theory and Practice*. Ithaca: Cornell University Press.
Sturm, Roland with Müller, Markus M. (1999) *Public Deficits. A Comparison of Their Political and Economic Consequences*. Harlow: Longman.
Sunstein, Cass R. (1990) *After the Rights Revolution: Reconceiving the Regulatory State*. Cambridge, Mass.: Harvard University Press.
Viscusi, W. Kip, Vernon, John M. & Harrington, Joseph E. (1996) *Economics of Regulation and Antitrust*. Cambridge, Mass.: MIT Press.
Vogel, Barbara (1983) *Allgemeine Gewerbefreiheit. Die Reformpolitik des preußischen Staatskanzlers Hardenberg (1810–1820)*. Göttingen: Vadenhoeck & Ruprecht.
Vogel, Steven K. (1996) *Freer Markets, More Rules. Regulatory Reform in Advanced Industrial Countries*. Ithaca: Cornell University Press.
Wagner, Adolph (1911) 'Der Staat in nationalökonomischer Sicht', *Handwörterbuch der Staatswissenschaften*. 3rd edition. Vol. VII. Jena: Fischer, pp. 727–739..
Wallerstein, Immanuel (1974) *The Modern World System: Capitalist Agriculture and the Origins of the European World conomy in the Sixteenth Century*. New York: Academic Press.

Weber, Max (1958) *The Protestant Ethic and the Spirit of Capitalism*. Translated by Talcott Parsons. New York: Scribners.
von Weizsäcker, Carl F. (1999) *Logik der Globalisierung*. Göttingen: Vandenhoeck & Ruprecht.
Whicker, Marcia Lynn (1993) *Controversial Issues in Economic Regulatory Policy*. Newbury Park: Sage.
Wilks, Stephen (1996) 'Regulatory Compliance and Capitalist Diversity in Europe', *Journal of European Public Policy* 3, no. 4, pp. 536–559.
Ziekow, Jan (1992) *Freiheit und Bindung des Gewerbes*. Berlin: Duncker & Humblot.
Zuckerman, Alan S. (1991) *Doing Political Science. An Introduction to Political Analysis*. Boulder: Westview Press

Telecommunications

Bauer, Brigitte (1996) *Verbraucherschutz und Wettbewerb in der Telekommunikation*. Berlin: Springer.
Benz, Angelika (1997) 'Privatisierung und Regulierung im Post- und Fernmeldewesen', in König, Klaus & Benz, Angelika (eds) *Privatisierung und staatliche Regulierung. Bahn, Post und Telekommunikation, Rundfunk*. Baden-Baden: Nomos, pp. 262–346.
Büchner, Wolfgang, Ehmer, Jörg, Geppert, Martin, Kerkhoff, Bärbel, Piepenbrock, Hermann-Josef, Schütz, Raimund & Schuster, Fabian (eds) *Beck'scher TKG-Kommentar*. München: Beck.
Bundesministerium für Post und Fernmeldewesen (1983) *Stellungnahme des Postministeriums (Referat 902) zum Abschlußbericht des Länderarbeitskreises "DBP und Fernmeldemonopol"*. Bonn: BMPF.
Bundesministerium für das Post- und Fernmeldewesen (1986) *Chance und Herausforderung der Telekommunikation in den 90er Jahren*. Bonn: BMPF.
Bundesministerium für Post und Fernmeldewesen (ed) (1987) *Eckpunkte für die Reform des Post- und Fernmeldewesens. Schwarz-Schilling vor dem 'Münchner Kreis'. Pressemitteilung des Bundesministeriums für Post und Fernmeldewesen v. 21.9.1987*. Bonn: BMPF.
Bundesministerium für Wirtschaft (1996) *Orientierungen für eine Postreform III. Gutachten des Wissenschaftlichen Beitrats beim Bundesministerium für Wirtschaft. Studienreihe des Bundesministeriums für Wirtschaft Nr. 85*. Bonn: BMWi.
Busch, Arnold (1983) *Die Deutsche Bundespost – Bremse des technischen Fortschritts. Arbeitspapier Nr. 191*. Kiel: Institut für Weltwirtschaft.
Ehring, Lothar (1999) 'Grundlagen und Entwicklung der Liberalisierung der Telekommunkationsmärkte in Europa – zugleich ein Beitrag zu Art. 90 EGV', Hoeren, Thomas & Queck, Robert (eds) *Rechtsfragen der Informationsgesellschaft*. Berlin: Duncker & Humblot, pp. 32–81.
Engel, Christoph & Knieps, Günter (1998) *Die Vorschriften des Telekommunikationsgesetzes über den Zugang zu wesentlichen Leistungen. Eine juristisch-ökonomische Untersuchung*. Baden-Baden: Nomos.
Geppert, Martin, Ruhle, Ernst-Olav & Schuster, Fabian (1998) *Handbuch Recht und Praxis der Telekommunikation*. Baden-Baden: Nomos..
Goumagias, Konstantinos (1998) *Die Stellung der Telekommunikation im Europäischen Vertrag*. Münster: Lit.

Gramlich, Ludwig (1994) 'Von der Postreform zur Postneuordnung', *Neue Juristische Wochenschrift* 43, pp. 2785–2793.
Gramlich, Ludwig (1997) 'Entwicklungen der staatlichen Wirtschaftsaufsicht: das Telekommunikationsrecht als Modell?' *Verwaltungsarchiv* 88, pp. 598–644.
Grande, Edgar (1989) *Vom Monopol zum Wettbewerb? Die neokonservative Reform der Telekommunikation in Großbritannien und der Bundesrepublik Deutschland.* Wiesbaden: Westdeutscher Verlag.
Haar, Brigitte (1995) *Marktöffnung in der Telekommunikation. Zum Verhältnis zwischen Wirtschaftsaufsicht und Normen gegen Wettbewerbsbeschränkungen im US-amerikanischen Recht, im europäischen Recht und im deutschen Recht.* Baden-Baden. Nomos.
Herrmann, Ernst (1985) 'Das Kräftespiel bei der Lenkung der Deutschen Bundespost. Verfassungswirklichkeit in einem öffentlichen Unternehmen', *Zeitschrift für öffentliche und gemeinwirtschaftliche Unternehmen* 8, pp. 285–300.
Hollingsworth, Rogers J., Schmitter, Philippe & Streeck, Wolfgang (eds) (1994) *Governing Capitalist Economies. Performance and Control of Economic Sectors.* New York: Oxford UP.
Jäger, Bernd (1994) *Postreform I und II. Die gradualistische Telekommunikationspolitik in Deutschland im Lichte der Positiven Theorie staatlicher Regulierung und Deregulierung.* Köln: Institut für Wirtschaftspolitik.
Klodt, Henning, Laaser, Claus-Friedrich, Lorz, Jens Oliver & Maurer, Rainer (1995) *Wettbewerb und Regulierung in der Telekommunikation.* Tübingen: Mohr.
Kühn, Dieter (1971) 'Die neue Unternehmensverfassung der Deutschen Bundespost', *Jahrbuch des Postwesens* 21, pp. 9–101.
Kühn, Dieter & Reimann, Wolfgang (1994) 'Einführung', Bundesministerium für Post und Telekommunikation (ed) *Postreform II. Gesetz zur Änderung des Grundgesetzes. Gesetz zur Neuordnung des Postwesens und der Telekommunikation. Text und Einführung.* Heidelberg: R. v. Decker's Verlag, G. Schenck, pp. 1–26.
Kuhn, Erich (1986) 'Überblick über die Entwicklung der ordnungspolitischen Diskussion im Bereich der Telekommunikation', *Zeitschrift für öffentliche und gemeinwirtschaftliche Unternehmen* 9, pp. 169–185.
Lehmbruch, Gustav (1981) 'Wandlungen der Interessenpolitik im liberalen Korporatismus', Alemann, Ulrich von & Heinze,Rolf G. (eds) *Verbände und Staat.* Opladen: Westdeutscher Verlag, pp. 50–71.
McKinsey & Company (1987) *Leistungsstandard, Tarife und Innovationsförderung im Fernmeldewesen. Gutachten im Auftrag der Regierungskommission Fernmeldewesen.* Bonn: BMPT.
Meierhofer, Hans (1997) 'Privatisierung und Regulierung aus der Sicht des Bundesamtes für Post und Telekommunikation als Regulierungsbehörde', in König, Klaus & Benz, Angelika (eds) *Privatisierung und staatliche Regulierung. Bahn, Post und Telekommunikation, Rundfunk.* Baden-Baden: Nomos, pp. 210–220.
van Miert, Karel (1998) 'Probleme der wettbewerblichen Öffnung von Märkten mit Netzstrukturen aus europäischer Sicht. Das Beispiel Telekommunikation', *Wirtschaft und Wettbewerb*, pp. 7–14.
Möschel, Weinhard (1988) 'Deregulierung in der Telekommunikation. Eine vergleichende Analyse des politischen Umfeldes', *ORDO* 39, pp. 173–182.
Monopolkommission (1981) *Die Rolle der Deutschen Bundespost im Fernmeldewesen. Sondergutachten der Monopolkommission gemäß § 24 b V Satz 4 GWB.* Band 9. Baden-Baden: Nomos.

Müller-Terpitz, Ralf (1997) 'Die Regulierungsbehörde für den Telekommunikationsmarkt', *Zeitschrift für Gesetzgebung* 12, pp. 257–274.

Neumann, Karl-Heinz (1991) 'Ökonomische Ziele der Regulierung der Telekommunikationsmärkte', BMPT (ed) *Regulierung und Wettbewerb in der Telekommunikation*. Informationsserie zu Regulierungsfragen Nr. 3. Bonn: BMPT, pp. 80–96.

North, Gottfried (1974) 'Die geschichtliche Entwicklung des Post- und Fernmeldewesens'. *Sonderdruck des Archivs für deutsche Postgeschichte* 2, pp. 6–25.

OECD (1987) *The Telecommunications Industry: The Challenges of Structural Change*. Report Prepared for the Structural Adjustment Project. Paris: OECD.

Ortwein, Edmund (1998) *Das Bundeskartellamt. Eine politische Ökonomie deutscher Wettbewerbspolitik*. Baden-Baden: Nomos.

Owen, Bruce M. & Braeutigam, R. (1978) *The Regulation Game. Strategic Use of the Administrative Process*. Cambridge, Mass.: Ballinger Publishing.

Paulweber, Michael (1999) *Regulierungszuständigkeiten in der Telekommunikation. Sektorspezifische Wettbewerbsaufsicht nach dem TKG durch die Regulierungsbehörde im Verhältnis zu den allgemeinen kartellrechtlichen Kompetenzen des Bundeskartellamtes und der Europäischen Kommission*. Baden-Baden: Nomos.

Rosenthal, Michael (1998) *Die Kompetenz der Europäischen Gemeinschaft für den rechtlichen Rahmen der Informationsgesellschaft*. Berlin: Duncker & Humblot.

Sachverständigenrat zur Begutachtung der gesamtwirtschaftlichen Entwicklung (1981) *Jahresgutachten 1981/82*. Stuttgart: Metzner.

Sachverständigenrat zur Begutachtung der gesamtwirtschaftlichen Entwicklung (1985) *Jahresgutachten 1985/86*. Stuttgart: Metzner.

Scherer, Joachim (1993) 'Rechtliche Instrumente und Verfahren zur Regulierung der Deutschen Bundespost Telekom vor und nach der Privatisierung', *Archiv für Post und Telekommunikation* 3, pp. 261–267.

Scherer, Joachim (1994) 'Postreform II: Privatisierung ohne Liberalisierung', *Computer & Recht* 7, pp. 418–426.

Scheuerle, Klaus-Dieter (1997) 'Privatisierung und Regulierung im Bereich Post und Telekommunikation', in König, Klaus & Benz, Angelika (eds) *Privatisierung und staatliche Regulierung. Bahn, Post und Telekommunikation, Rundfunk*. Baden-Baden: Nomos, pp. 201–209.

Schneider, Volker & Werle, Raymund (1989) *Governance by Policy Networks: The German Telecommunications Sector*. Köln: MPI.

Schwintowski, Hans-Peter (1997) 'Ordnung und Wettbewerb auf Telekommunikationsmärkten', *Computer & Recht*, pp. 630–638.

Sondhof, Harald (1994) *Telekommunikation nach der Privatisierung – Liberalisierung und Wettbewerb*. Diskussionsbeitrag Nr. 38. Tübingen: Wirtschaftswissenschaftliches Seminar.

Voeth, Markus (1996) *Entmonopolisierung von Märkten – Das Beispiel Telekommunikation*. Baden-Baden: Nomos.

Webber, David (1986) 'Die ausbleibende Wende bei der Deutschen Bundespost. Zur Regulierung des Telekommunikationswesens in der Bundesrepublik Deutschland', *Politische Vierteljahresschrift* 27 (1986), pp. 397–450.

Werle, Raymund (1990) *Telekommunikation in der Bundesrepublik. Expansion, Differenzierung, Transformation*. Frankfurt a. M.. Campus.

Witte, Eberhard (ed) (1987) *Neuordnung der Telekommunikation. Bericht der Regierungskommission Fernmeldewesen*. Heidelberg: R.v. Decker's.

Ziegler, J. Nicholas (1999) *Technologiepolitik. Innovationsstrategien in Deutschland und Frankreich.* Frankfurt a. M.: Campus.
Zydorek, Christoph (1998) *Soziale Steuerung und Koordination in der Telekommunikation. Eine sozialwissenschaftliche Analyse.* Baden-Baden: Nomos.

Broadcasting

Albert, Reinhold (1997) 'Entwicklung der Privatisierung und Regulierung im Bereich des Rundfunks', in König, Klaus & Benz, Angelika (eds) *Privatisierung und statliche Regulierung. Bahn, Post und Telekommunikation, Rundfunk.* Baden-Baden: Nomos, pp. 347–56.
ARD (ed) (1980) 'Rundfunkpolitik 1979', *ARD-Jahrbuch 80.* Hamburg: Hans-Bredow-Institut, pp. 101–10.
Bauer, Thomas (1993) *Deutsche Programmpresse 1923 bis 1941. Entstehung, Entwicklung und Kontinuität der Rundfunkzeitschriften.* München: Saur.
Bausch, Hans (1983) 'Ein neues Medium wird 60 Jahre alt. Zwischen wechselvoller Geschichte und offener Zukunft', Arbeitsgemeinschaft der öffentlich-rechtlichen Rundfunkanstalten der Bundesrepublik Deutschland (ARD) (Hrsg) *ARD-Jahrbuch 83.* Hamburg: Verlag Hans-Bredow-Institut, pp. 19–40.
Bausch, Hans (1975) 'Zweieinhalb Jahrzehnte Rundfunkpolitik. Resümee anläßlich des Jubiläums der ARD', ARD (Hrsg) *ARD-Jahrbuch 1975.* Hamburg: Verlag Hans-Bredow-Institut, pp. 18–37.
Benz, Angelika (1997) 'Privatisierung und Regulierung im Rundfunk', in König, Klaus & Benz, Angelika (eds) *Privatisierung und staatliche Regulierung. Bahn, Post und Telekommunikation, Rundfunk.* Baden-Baden: Nomos, pp. 419–536.
Bethge, Herbert (1987) 'Verfassungstreue für private Rundfunkveranstalter?' *Neue Juristische Wochenschrift* 40, pp. 2982–2984.
Bethge, Herbert (1995) 'Rundfunkgesetzgebung. Thematik, Trends, Tendenzen', *Zeitschrfit für Gesetzgebung* 10, pp. 101–131.
Bethge, Herbert (1997) 'Rechtliche Fragen der Privatisierung und Regulierung des Rundfunks', in König, Klaus & Benz, Angelika (Hrsg) *Privatisierung und staatliche Regulierung. Bahn, Post und Telekommunikation, Rundfunk.* Baden-Baden: Nomos, pp. 387–405.
Degenhart, Christoph (1987) 'Bayern auf dem Weg zur Dualen Rundfunkordnung? Bayerisches Medienerprobungs- und -entwicklungsgesetz, Bayerische Verfassung und Grundgesetz. Zur Entscheidung des BayVerfGH vom 21.11.1986', *Archiv für Presserecht* 18, pp. 371–375.
Diller, Ansgar (1975) '25 Jahre ARD. Ausgewählte Daten und Fakten', ARD (Hrsg) *ARD-Jahrbuch 75.* Hamburg: Verlag Hans-Bredow-Institut, pp.38–57.
Diller, Ansgar (1980) *Rundfunkpolitik im Dritten Reich.* München: DTV.
Direktorenkonferenz der Landesmedienanstalten (DLM) (ed) (1988) *DLM-Jahrbuch 88.* München: Neue Mediengesellschaft.
Dyson, Kenneth & Humphreys, Peter (1988) 'The Regulatory Change in Western Europe', Dyson, Kenneth & Humphreys, Peter (eds) *Broadcasting and New Media Policies in Western Europe.* London: Routledge, pp. 92–160.
Eberle, Carl-Eugen (1989) *Rundfunkübertragung.* Berlin: Duncker & Humblot.
Eberle, Carl-Eugen (1997) 'Privatisiserung und Regulierung aus der Sicht öffentlich-

rechtlicher Programmveranstalter', in König, Klaus & Benz, Angelika (Hrsg) *Privatisierung und staatliche Regulierung. Bahn, Post und Telekommunikation, Rundfunk.* Baden-Baden: Nomos, pp. 357–370.

Fromm, Michael (1998) *Öffentlich-rechtlicher Programmauftrag und Rundfunkföderalismus. Der verfassungsrechtliche Programmauftrag der Rundfunkanstalten unter besonderer Berücksichtigung des Rundfunkfinanzausgleichs.* Baden-Baden: Nomos.

Führer, Karl Christian (1997) *Wirtschaftsgeschichte des Rundfunks in der Weimarer Republik.* Potsdam: Verlag für Berlin-Brandenburg.

Gersdorf, Hubertus (1991) *Staatsfreiheit des Rundfunks in der dualen Rundfunkordnung der Bundesrepublik Deutschland.* Berlin: Duncker & Humblot.

Halefeldt, Horst O. (1989) 'Eckpfeiler der Demokratie. Die Errichtung öffentlich-rechtlicher Rundfunkanstalten vor 40 Jahren', Arbeitsgemeinschaft der öffentlich-rechtlichen Rundfunkanstalten der Bundesrepublik Deutschland (ARD) *ARD-Jahrbuch 89.* Hamburg: Hans-Bredow-Institut Verlag, pp.19–24.

Hecker, Wolfgang (1987) 'Das 4. Rundfunkurteil des Bundesverfassungsgerichts', *Demokratie und Recht* 15, pp. 65–78..

Hellstern, Gerd-Michael & Reese, Jürgen (eds) (1989) *Ziele. Organisation und Leistung der Landesmedienanstalten für Rundfunk. Bd. 16/1–111 der Begleitforschung des Landes Nordrhein-Westfalen zum Kabelpilotprojekt Dortmund.* Düsseldorf: Presse- und Informationsdienst der Landesregierung Nordrhein-Westfalen.

Herres, Volker & Plog, Jobst (1989) 'Ständige Systemveränderung. 40 Jahre Rundfunkgesetzgebung', ARD (ed) *ARD-Jahrbuch 89.* Hamburg: Verlag Hans-Bredow-Institut, pp. 25–38.

Herrmann, Günter (1975) *Fernsehen und Hörfunk in der Verfassung der Bundesrepublik Deutschland. Zugleich ein Beitrag zur weiteren allgemeinen verfassungsrechtlichen und kommunikationsrechtlichen Fragen.* Tübingen: Mohr.

Hillig, Hans-Peter (1990) 'Das Europäische Übereinkommen über das grenzüberschreitende Fernsehen und die EG-Fernsehrichtlinie', ARD (ed) *ARD-Jahrbuch 90.* Hamburg: Verlag Hans-Bredow-Institut, pp. 417–432.

Hoffmann, Martin (1995) 'Programmquoten und Werbebegrenzungen als Gegenstand des Aufsichtsrechts im Rundfunk', Mestmäcker, ERnst-Joachim (ed) *Kommunikation ohne Monopole II. Ein Symposium über Ordnungsprinzipien im Wirtschaftsrecht der Telekommunikation und der elektronischen Medien.* Baden-Baden: Nomos, pp. 607– 638.

Hoffmann-Riem, Wolfgang (1991) 'Rundfunk als public service – ein überholtes Konzept? Weiß, Ralph (ed) *Aufgaben und Perspektiven des öffentlich-rechtlichen Fernsehens.* Baden-Baden: Nomos, pp. 21–47.

Hoffmann-Riem, Wolfgang (1991a) *Rundfunkrecht neben Wirtschaftsrecht. Zur Anwendbarkeit des GWB und des EWG-V auf das Wettbewerbsverhalten öffentlich-rechtlichen Rundfunks in der dualen Rundfunkordnung.* Baden-Baden: Nomos.

Hoffmann-Riem, Wolfgang (1995) *Licensing and Supervision of Broadcasting. Experiences in Six Countries.* Hamburg: Verlag Hans-Bredow-Institut.

Holznagel, Bernd (1996) *Rundfunkecht in Europa.* Tübingen: Mohr.

Humphreys, Peter J. (1994) 'Media and Media Policy in Germany'. *The Press and Broadcasting since 1945.* Oxford: Berg.

Kaiser, Ulrike (1989) 'Fest verzahnt. Rundfunkaufsicht zwischen Politik und Medienwirtschaft', *Der Journalist* 8, pp. 8–15.

Keidel, Hannemor (1993) 'Politische Aspekte der öffentlich-rechtlichen Rundfunkaufsicht über Privatfunkprogramme in Bayern', Jarren, Otfried,

Marcinkowski, Frank & Schatz, Heribert (eds) *Landesmedienanstalten – Steuerung der Rundfunkentwicklung? Jahrbuch 1993 der Arbeitskreise „Politik und Kommunikation" der DVPW und der DGPuk*. Münster: LIT Verlag, pp. 97–110.

Kirschnek, Oliver (1998) *Landesmediengesetz Baden-Württemberg. Verfassungsrechtliche Grundprinzipien und Probleme*. Berlin: Duncker & Humblot.

Kleinsteuber, Hans J. (1993) 'Vom Bundesverfassungsgericht zu den Landesmedienanstalten', Jarren, Otfrie, Marcinkowski, Frank & Schatz, Heribert (eds) *Landesmedienanstalten – Steuerung der Rundfunkentwicklung? Jahrbuch 1993 der Arbeitskreise „Politik und Kommunikation" der DVPW und der DGPuK*. Münster: LIT Verlag, pp. 23–48.

Kreile, Johannes (1997) 'Die Reform des Rundfunkstaatsvertrags – Neue Wege bei der Vielfaltssicherung im privaten Rundfunk', *Neue Juristische Wochenschrift* 50, pp. 1329–1334.

Lammek, Marc (1997) *Die Kooperation der Landesmedienanstalten*. Frankfurt a. M.: Lang.

Lehment, Cornelius (1996) *Rundfunkfreiheit und Finanzkontrolle. Zur Rechnungsprüfung bei den öffentlich-rechtlichen Rundfunkanstalten und den Landesmedienanstalten*. Frankfurt a.M.: Peter Lang.

Lerg, Winfried B. (1970) 'Die Entstehung des Rundfunks in Deutschland'. *Herkunft und Entwicklung eines publizistischen Mittels*. Frankfurt a.M.: Knecht.

Libertus, Michael (1991) *Grundversorgungsauftrag und Funktionsgarantie*. München: Beck.

Maassen, Ludwig (1979) *Der Kampf um den Rundfunk in Bayern. Rundfunkpolitik in Bayern 1945–1973*. Berlin: Spiess.

Merznicht, Roman (1992) *Der „Aufsichtsgroschen". Die verfassungsrechtliche Problematik der Finanzierung der Zulassungs- und Aufsichtsfunktionen der Landesmedienanstalten aus der Rundfunkgebühr*. München: Verlag V. Florentz.

Mestmäcker, Ernst Joachim et al. (1990) *Der Einfluß des europäischen Gemeinschaftsrechts auf die deutsche Rundfunkordnung*. Baden-Baden: Nomos.

Neuffer, Martin (1975) 'Der Rundfunkintendant. Selbstverständnis, Funktionen, Aufgaben', ARD (ed) *ARD-Jahrbuch 75*. Hamburg. Verlag Hans-Bredow-Institut, pp. 81–89.

Neugebauer, Eberhard (1929) *Fernmelderecht und Rundfunkrecht*. Berlin, pp. 748–791.

Neupert, Helmuth (1997) 'Privatisierung und Regulierung aus der Sicht der Landesmedienanstalten', in König, Klaus & Benz, Angelika (eds) *Privatisierung und staatliche Regulierung. Bahn, Post und Telekommunikation, Rundfunk*. Baden-Baden: Nomos, pp. 371–386.

Niepalla, Peter (1990) *Die Grundversorgung durch die öffentlich-rechtlichen Rundfunkanstalten*. München: Beck.

Niewiarra, Manfred (1989) 'Die rechtlichen, politischen, technischen und ökonomischen Rahmenbedingungen für das Eindringen der privatwirtschaftlichen Medienkonzerne in den Bereich der öffentlich-rechtlichen elektronischen Medien', in Röper, Burkhardt (ed) *Wettbewerbsprobleme öffentlich- und privatrechtlicher Medien*. Berlin: Duncker & Humblot, pp. 13–31.

Oeller, Helmut (1989) 'Das Programm und die Produzenten. Tatsachen und Perspektiven', in Röper, Burkhardt (ed) *Wettbewerbsprobleme öffentlich- und privatrechtlicher Medien*. Berlin: Duncker & Humblot, pp.111–120.

Preuss Neudorf, Friedrich Christian (1993) *Grundversorgung und Wettbewerb im dualen Rundfunksystem – Medienrechtliche und wettbewerbsrechtliche Aspekte*. Frankfurt a.M.: Lang.

Reichs-Rundfunk-Gesellschaft (RRG) (1926) *Geschäftsbericht über das Geschäftsjahr*

1925/1926. Anlage zum Protokoll der RRG-Gesellschafterversammlung, 7.9.1926. Berlin.

Reichs-Rundfunk-Gesellschaft (RRG) (1927) *Geschäftsbericht über das Geschäftsjahr 1926/27*. Anlage zum Protokoll der RRG-Gesellschafterversammlung, 15.6.1927. Berlin.

Reichs-Rundfunk-Gesellschaft (RRG) (1929) *Geschäftsbericht über das vierte Geschäftsjahr 1928*. Berlin.

Reichs-Rundfunk-Gesellschaft (RRG) (1930) *Geschäftsbericht über das fünfte Geschäftsjahr 1930*. Berlin.

Reichs-Rundfunk-Gesellschaft (RRG) (1932) *Geschäftsbericht über das siebente Geschäftsjahr 1931. Bilanz mit Gewinn- und Verlustrechnung für 1931. Haushaltsplan für 1932*. Berlin.

Rossen, Helge (1992) 'Öffentlich-rechtlicher Rundfunk in den fünf neuen Ländern', in Hans-Bredow-Institut (ed) *Das Rundfunkrecht der neuen Bundesländer. Eine kommentierte Dokumentation*. Baden-Baden: Nomos, pp. 9–58.

Scharf, Albert (1996) 'Vernetzen statt versparten. Die ARD im Trialen Rundfunksystem', in ARD (ed) *ARD-Jahrbuch 96*. Hamburg: Verlag Hans-Bredow-Institut, pp. 13–15.

Schmücker, Rainulf (1969) 'Unabhängigkeit und Einheit. Wie die ARD entstanden ist', ARD (Hrsg) *ARD-Jahrbuch 69*. Hamburg: Verlag Hans-Bredow-Institut, pp. 19–49.

Schmücker, Rainulf (1970) 'Neue Rundfunkstruktur in Südwestdeutschland? Das Problem ist 20 Jahre alt', in ARD (ed) *ARD-Jahrbuch 70*. Hamburg: Verlag Hans-Bredow-Institut, pp. 18–31.

Schmücker, Rainulf (1973) 'Auch ein 50-Jahr-Jubiläum. Die Leistungen der Post für den Rundfunk und die Entgelte', in ARD (ed) *ARD-Jahrbuch 73*. Hamburg: Verlag Hans-Bredow-Institut, pp. 41–72.

Schuler-Harms, Margarete (1992) 'Privatfunkregulierung in den neuen Bundesländern', in Hans-Bredow-Institut (ed) *Das Rundfunkrecht der neuen Bundesländer. Eine kommentierte Dokumentation*. Baden-Baden: Nomos, pp. 59–73.

Schuler-Harms, Margarete (1995) *Rundfunkaufsicht im Bundesstaat. Die Arbeitsgemeinschaft der Landesmedienanstalten*. Baden-Baden: Nomos.

Smend, Rudolf (1928) *Verfassung und Verfassungsrecht*. München: Duncker & Humblot.

Steininger, Rolf (1975) 'Rundfunkpolitik im ersten Kabinett Adenauer', in Lerg, Winfried B. &Steininger, Rolf (eds) *Rundfunk und Politik. 1923 – 1973*. Berlin: Spiess, pp. 341–384.

Stock, Martin (1997) 'Meinungsvielfalt und Meinungsmacht. Das duale Rundfunksystem nach der staatsvertraglichen Neuregelung (1996)', *Juristenzeitung* 52, pp. 583–595.

Thieme, Werner (1963) 'Der Finanzausgleich im Rundfunkwesen', *Archiv des öffentlichen Rechts* 88, pp. 38–80.

Vahrenhold, Olaf (1992) *Die Stellung der Privatfunkaufsicht im System staatlicher Aufsicht*. Baden-Baden: Nomos.

Vollmann, Heinz (1936) *Rechtlich-wirtschaftlich-soziologische Grundlagen der deutschen Rundfunkentwicklung. Eine umfassende Darstellung aller die Rundfunkeinheit betreffenden Probleme in Vergangenheit, Gegenwart und Zukunft*. Borna-Leipzig, p. 29–30.

Wagner, Christoph (1990) *Die Landesmedienanstalten. Organisation und Verfahren der Kontrolle privater Rundfunkveranstalter in der Bundesrepublik Deutschland*. Baden-Baden: Nomos.

Ziethen, Michael P. (1989) 'Rechtliche Spielräume der Lizenzierung und Kontrolle – ausgewählte Regelungsfelder', in Hellstern, Gerd-Michael & Reese, Jürgen (eds) (1989) *Ziele. Organisation und Leistung der Landesmedienanstalten für Rundfunk.* Bd. 16/111 der Begleitforschung des Landes Nordrhein-Westfalen zum Kabelpilotprojekt Dortmund. Düsseldorf: Presse- und Informationsdienst der Landesregierung Nordrhein-Westfalen, pp. 59– 161.

Zuck, Rüdiger (1999) 'Viel Lärm – um nichts? Nachdenken über die ARD', *Neue Juristische Wochenschrift* 48, pp. 1331–1333.

Banking

Amely, Tobias (1994) *Allfinanz-Konzerne als Problem der Bank- und Versicherungsaufsicht. Vorschläge zu einer integrativen Behandlung der Erfolgsrisiken.* Köln: Botermann & Botermann, pp. 259–262.

Bähre, Inge Lore & Schneider, Manfred (1986) *KWG-Kommentar. Kreditwesengesetz mit den wichtigsten Ausführungsvorschriften.* München: Beck.

Becker, Wolf-Dieter (1983) 'Regulierungsprobleme im Bankgewerbe', in Thiemeyer, Th. (ed) *Öffentliche Bindung von Unternehmen. Beiträge zur Regulierungsdebatte. Gert von Eynern zum 80. Geburtstag.* Baden-Baden: Nomos, pp. 309–323.

Bieg, Hartmut (1983) *Bankbilanzen und Bankenaufsicht.* München: Beck.

Blumer, Andreas (1996) *Bankenaufsicht und Bankenprüfung. Grundkonzepte, Problembestand und Perspektiven der institutionellen Ausgestaltung ausgewählter Bankenüberwachungssysteme.* Bern: Paul Haupt.

Burghof, Hans-Peter & Rudolph, Bernd (1996) *Bankenaufsicht. Theorie und Praxis der Regulierung.* Wiesbaden: Gabler.

Born, Karl Erich (1967) *Die deutsche Bankenkrise 1931. Finanzen und Politik.* München: Piper.

Down, Kevin (1992a) 'Models of Banking Instability: A Partial Review of the Literature', *Journal of Economic Surveys* 6, pp. 107–132.

Dürre, Günter (1974) 'Kann das Aufsichtsamt Bankinsolvenzen verhindern?' *Österreichisches Bankarchiv* 22, pp. 186–195.

Fischer, Otfried (1975) 'Funktion und Wirkungsweise der Liquiditäts-Konsortialbank GmbH', *Österreichisches Bank-Archiv* 23, pp. 2-8.

Fischer, Reinfrid & Klanten, Thomas (2000) *Bankrecht. Grundlagen der Rechtspraxis.* Köln: RWS.

Geiger, Helmut (1984) 'KWG-Reform und Überlegungen zum SMH-Fall', *Die Sparkasse* 101, pp. 7–10.

Grundmann, Wolfgang (1992) 'Die Einlagensicherungssysteme', *Zeitschrift für das gesamte Kreditwesen* 45, pp. 1134–1138.

Günther, Hans (1975) 'Die künfitge Einlagensicherung der privaten Banken', *Bankbetrieb* 14, pp. 250–252.

Hellenthal, Ludger (1992) *Das Bankenaufsichtsrecht der Europäischen Gemeinschaft.* Berlin: Duncker & Humblot.

Herrhausen, Alfred (1989) 'Die Wettbewerbsposition der deutschen Universalbanken im europäischen Binnenmarkt', in Kolbeck, Rosemarie (ed) *Chancen und Risiken der deutschen Banken im Gemeinsamen Markt.* Frankfurt a. M.: Knapp, pp. 79–94.

Hütz, Gerhard (1990) *Die Bankenaufsicht in der Bundesrepublik Deutschland und in den*

USA: Ein Rechtsvergleich. Berlin: Duncker & Humblot, pp. 20–45..
Kindermann, Elmar (1987) 'Zur Rechtfertigung der kreditwirtschaftlichen Bereichsausnahme nach § 102 KWG', in Helmrich, Herbert (ed) *Wettbewerbspolitik und Wettbewerbsrecht*. Köln: Heymanns, pp. 277–298.
Kokemoor, Axel (1997) *Die Bankaufsicht auf konsolidierter Basis in Deutschland nach der fünften Novelle zum KWG: Mit Ausblick auf die Änderungen der sechsten Novelle*. Bayreuth: P.C.O..
Kratzner, Jakob (1950) 'Die Bundesoberbehörde', *Die öffentliche Verwaltung* 3, pp. 529–536.
Krümmel, Hans J. (1984) 'Schutzzweck und Aufsichtseingriffe', *Kredit und Kapital* 17, pp. 474–488 .
Kuntze, Wolfgang (1985) 'Die Beaufsichtigung der Kreditinstitute auf konsolidierter Basis nach dem Dritten KWG-Änderungsgesetz', in Förster, Karl-Heinz (ed) *Beiträge zur Bankaufsicht, Bankbilanz und Bankprüfung. Unter Berücksichtigung der Dritten KWG-Novelle. Dr. Walter Scholz zum 65. Geburtstag*. Düsseldorf: IDW, pp. 119–136.
Kuntze, Wolfgang (1988) 'Bankenaufsicht als Verbraucherschutz?' *Bank und Markt* 17, pp. 5–12.
Lüke, Rolf E. (1981) *13. Juli 1931. Das Geheimnis der deutschen Bankenkrise*. Frankfurt a. M.: Knapp .
Möschel, Weinhard (1985) 'Eine Systematik von Bankenregulierungszielen', in Lutter, Marcus *et al.* (eds) *Festschrift für Walter Stimpel zum 68. Geburtstag am 29. November 1985*. Berlin: Duncker & Humblot, pp. 1065–85.
Müller, Andreas J. (1996a) *Bankenzulassung und -aufsicht in der Europäischen Union und den Vereinigten Staaten von Amerika*. Berlin: Papyrus.
Niethammer, Thomas (1990) *Die Ziele der Bankenaufsicht in der Bundesrepublik Deutschland. Das Verhältnis zwischen 'Gläubigerschutz' und 'Sicherung der Funktionsfähigkeit des Kreditwesen'*. Berlin: Duncker & Humblot.
Nirk, Rudolf (1996) *Das Kreditwesengesetz. Einführung und Kommentar*. Frankfurt a. M.: Knapp.
Oberbillig, Werner (1955) 'Bankenaufsicht - zentral oder dezentral?' *Zeitschrift für das gesamte Kreditgewerbe* 8, pp. 554–556.
Osthues, Heinz (1980) 'Die Ergebnisse des Berichts der Bankenstrukturkommission', *Die Sparkasse* 97, pp. 6–10.
Pecchioli, Rinaldo M. (1989) *Bankenaufsicht in den OECD-Ländern: Entwicklungen und Probleme*. Baden-Baden: Nomos.
Pleyer, Klemens (1988) *Bankkrisen und die Vorgeschichte der Bankenaufsicht von der Reichsgewerbeordnung bis zum Reichsgesetz über das Kreditwesen von 1934*. Köln: Botermann & Botermann.
Puckler, Godehard (1974) 'Angemessene Bankaufsicht – Überwachung der Eigenkapitalausstattung und der Liquidität in Deutschland und den USA', *Die Wirtschaftsprüfung* 27, pp. 569–572.
Regnery, Peter (1994) *Bankenaufsicht, Bankeneigenkapital und Wettbewerb. Die Eigenkapitaldefinition nach der Vierten KWG-Novelle und der Einfluß auf die Wettbewerbsfähigkeit deutscher Kreditinstitute*. Stuttgart: Schäffer-Poeschel.
Reimnitz, Christoph (1992) *Der deutsche Eigenkapitalbegriff als Qualitätsbegriff. Eine grundlegende Analyse des § 10 KWG vor dem Hintergrund internationaler Harmonisierungsbestrebungen*. Wiesbaden: Gabler.
Römer, Monika (1977) *Harmonisierung der Bankenaufsicht in der EG*. Berlin: Duncker & Humblot.

Ronge, Volker (1979) *Bankpolitik im Spätkapitalismus. Politische Selbstverwaltung des Kapitals*. Frankfurt a. M.: Campus.

Schmidt, Dirk (1974) 'Lehren aus dem Herstatt-Fall', *Zeitschrift für das gesamte Kreditwesen* 27, pp. 665–666.

Schneider, Manfred (1978) *Praxis der Bankenaufsicht*. Frankfurt a.M.: Knapp.

Schork, Ludwig (1957) 'Die Auswirkungen des Gesetzes gegen Wettbewerbsbeschränkungen auf das Kreditwesen', *Sparkasse* 73, pp. 267–270.

Schork, Ludwig (1964) 'Die allgemeinen Maßnahmen des Bundesaufsichtsamtes für das Kreditwesen', *Der Bankbetrieb* 4, pp. 35–37.

Seifert, Ekkehart (1984) *Privilegien und Regulierung im Bankwesen. Ein Beitrag zur ordnungspolitischen Problematik branchenorientierter Strukturpolitik*. Baden-Baden: Nomos.

Starke, Otto-Ernst (1979) 'Das Gutachten der Bankenstrukturkommission und die Kreditwirtschaft', *Die Betriebswirtschaft* 39, pp. 543–550.

Stein, Ekkehart (1967) *Die Wirtschaftsaufsicht*. Tübingen: Mohr.

Steinert, Herbert (1955) 'Die Bankenaufsicht als Problem des Verwaltungsrechts und der Verwaltungspraxis', *Schmollers Jahrbuch für Gesetzgebung, Verwaltung und Volkswirtschaft*, pp. 63–98.

Stobbe, Susanne (1993) *Die deutsche Kreditwirtschaft im europäischen Bankenrecht. Bestandsaufnahme und Auswirkungen der Harmonisierungsbestrebungen auf den bundesdeutschen Bankensektor*. Frankfurt a. M.: Peter Lang.

Welcker, Johannes (1978) *Neuordnung der Bankenaufsicht*. Frankfurt a. M.: Knapp.

Zimmer, Klaus (1993) *Bankenregulierung: Zur Begründung und Ausgestaltung der Einlagensicherung. Eine ordnungstheoretische Analyse auf der Grundlage der Modernen Institutionenökonomik*. Baden-Baden: Nomos.

Index